a **FUN 4 FANS** special

Spirit of the '60s:
A Pop Culture Photo Album...

Jon Abbott

ISBN-13:978-1987702354

ISBN-10:1987702352

© Jon Abbott 2018

Also by Jon Abbott

Irwin Allen Television Productions, 1964-1970: A Critical History of Voyage to the Bottom of the Sea, Lost in Space, The Time Tunnel, and Land of the Giants
McFarland, 2006

The Elvis Films
Createspace Independent Publ., 2014

Cool TV of the 1960s: Three Shows That Changed the World
The Man from UNCLE, Batman, and The Monkees
Createspace Independent Publ., 2015

Strange New World: Sex Films of the 1970s
Createspace Independent Publ., 2015

The Great Desilu Series of the 1960s
The Untouchables, The Lucy Show, Star Trek, Mission: Impossible
Createspace Independent Publ., due 2016

for further details and more titles search Jon Abbott on Amazon

contents

introduction	005
Batman and Batmania	007
Doctor Who and Dalekmania	025
The Elvis Films	050
Gerry Anderson and Super-Marionation	067
Irwin Allen at 20th Century Fox	089
"Only in the '60s" Movies	126
about the author	134
other books by Jon Abbott	137

These pictures are presented as 'found history' and may yet perform their original function as promotional aids for their products in this book. I certainly hope so. As with all my writing and publications, the purpose is to generate and retain interest in these wonderful films and series, most now over fifty years old, as am I!

All characters and concepts are copyright their respective owners, studios and distributors, and there is no intent to infringe on any rights. We all want the same thing, to see these shows find their audience. Every once in a while, they do.

With thanks to the *Irwin Allen News Network* (find them on the net), the *Elvis Information Network* (ditto), my colleague Mark Phillips in Canada, who is always sending me images and undoubtedly contributed a couple herein, and to my many friends and contacts in the various program buying and selling departments during my 'TV news' days in the '80s and '90s. Retired and missing ya.

Apologies to anyone I've forgotten to credit. Sometimes even I forget where this stuff came from...

introduction

Elvis, *Batman, Lost in Space, Thunderbirds, Doctor Who*... Just the tip of the iceberg. What a decade for popular culture. Here are some rare and candid images from the era, some meticulously posed, some randomly snapped, all of them absolutely fascinating and evocative of the period.

I've been collecting and writing about 20th century pop culture for most of my life, and present here a lively, esoteric and eclectic collection of pictures and product I've retrieved from boot fairs, collectors' markets, and even programme distributors' rubbish bins during my trawl through the past for the present. I've gone out of my way to present the most bizarre and peculiar shots I've found over the years. All of them have been chosen to capture the particular mood of the times; they could not belong to any other decade. They are presented *mostly* without comment, and in some cases are a mystery even to me!

My books which are predominantly photos are not available on kindle because, quite frankly, this sort of publication doesn't transfer very well. If I ever find out a way to do it without compromising on quality, I will. But there's something to be said for the pocket book format.

Ian Fleming, whose hardback versions of James Bond's exploits were not too successful, but who in the paperback form inaugurated a whole new genre of then contemporary and modern Eurospy books in paperback, put it best when he said "They (the Bond novels) are written for warm-blooded heterosexuals in railways, hotels, aeroplanes, or beds". These slimline paperbacks are then, to take inspiration and explanation from Fleming, for the briefcase, the bedside table, the coffee table, the garden shed or garage, the bottom of the desk drawer for the office where the boss forbids internet access, for the lunchbox or train journey home, or sliding into the pocket in your car door. The color in these books does add to the price, but is essential, surely.

If *Spirit of the '60s* is successful, I have some neat ideas for a follow-up or two, so here's hoping. In the meantime, if you prefer something a little text-heavier, there's a plethora of hefty tomes on the '60s and the '70s (and even a couple on the '80s) advertised in the back pages. I've been doing this for a long time! Check out my author's page on amazon.com and Amazon.co.uk. Anyway, I shall close by saying what I always say: reviews do seem to count on Amazon, so if you like my books, please say so. If you don't, at least be fair. Don't be *that* guy! Unlike many on Amazon, I don't write my own reviews, because I figure if I can spot the fakeys, so can everyone else! So a good one is always, always appreciated.

Love and kisses,

Jon

Batman (and Batmania)

The Bat (1926) (or possibly, the remake The Bat Whispers, 1930), but either way without a doubt Bob Kane's main source of inspiration for you-know-who.

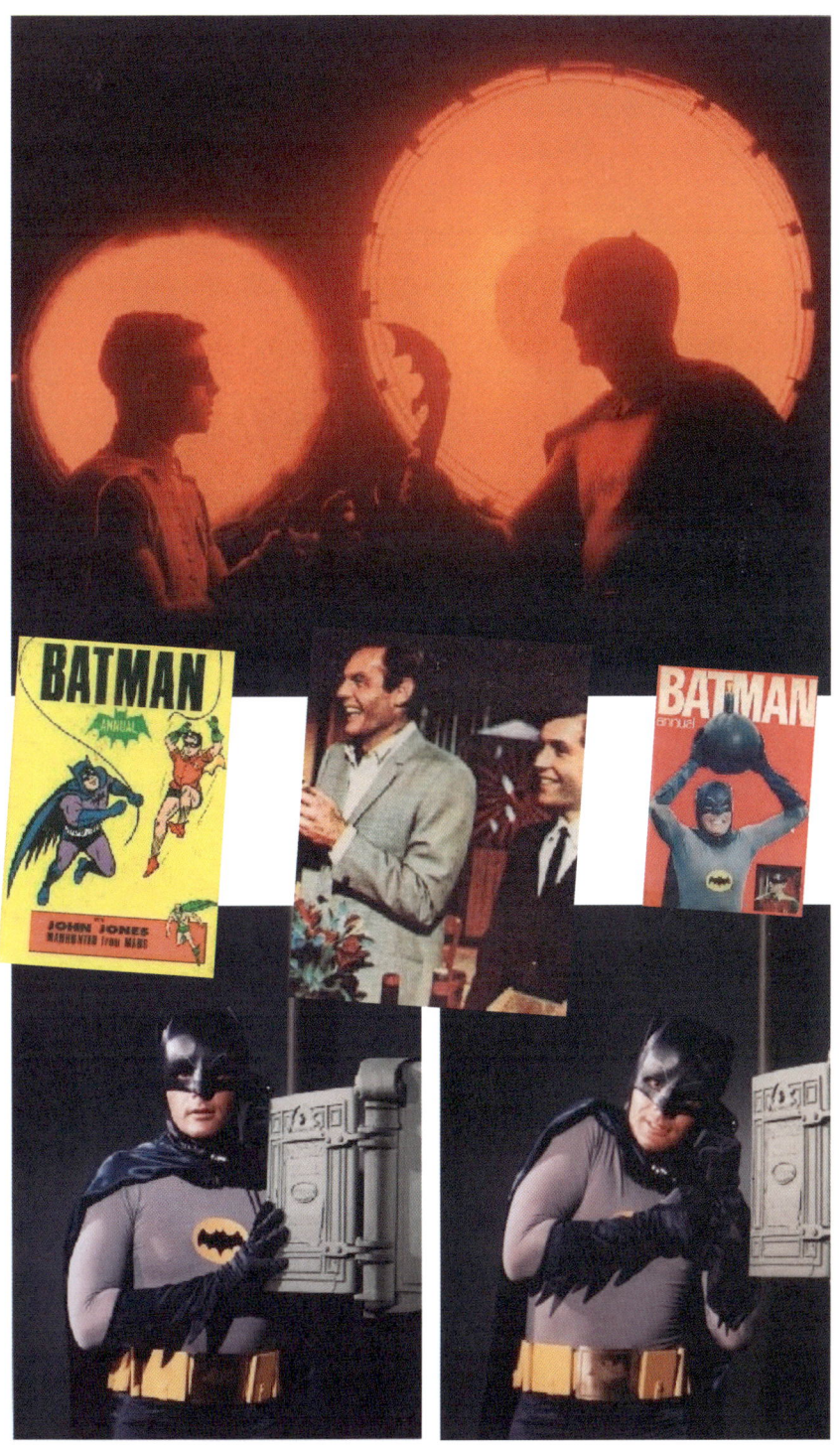

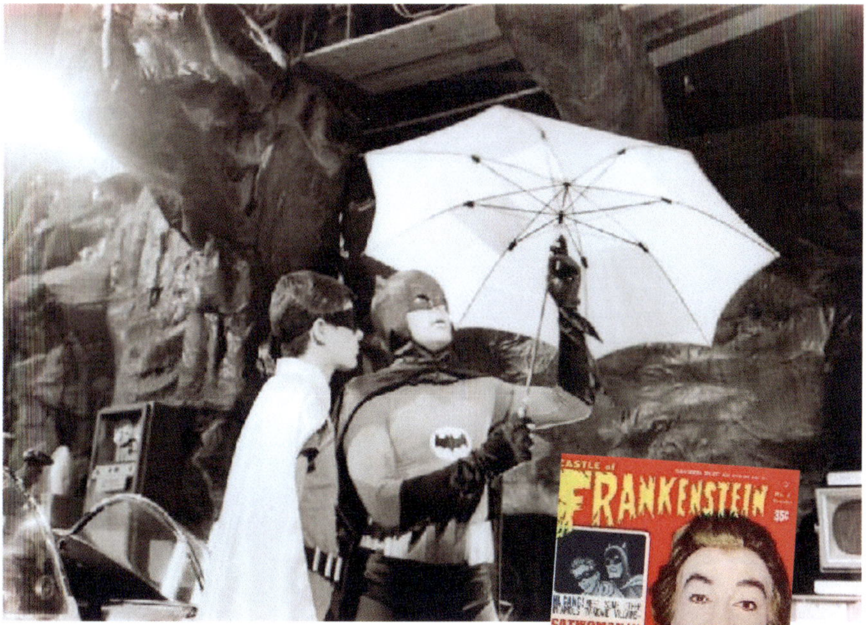

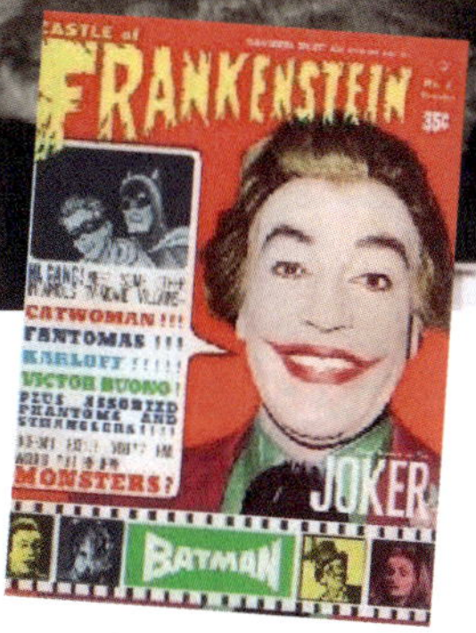

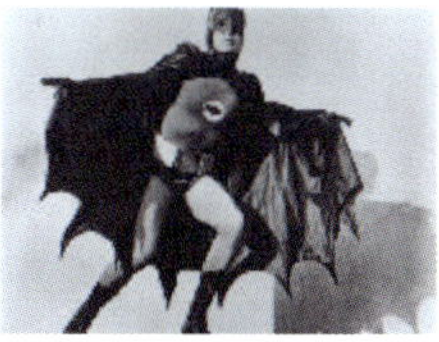

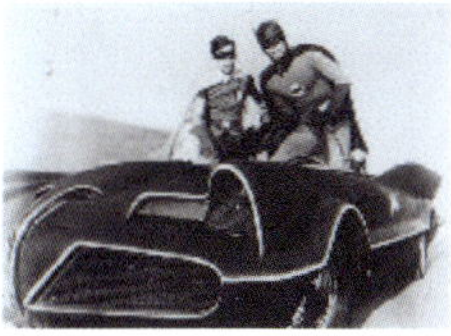

"You'll never guess who's on the 'phone next to me…"

Julie Newmar as the Catwoman

Left, Burt Ward in the Batboat with stunt driver Batman, below, on the soundstage with Adam West.

Burgess Meredith, Frank Gorshin, Lee Meriwether, Cesar Romero.

Frank Gorshin with Sherry Jackson and Linda Gaye Scott; Adam West with Yvonne Craig (in original Batgirl mask on library set for test footage).

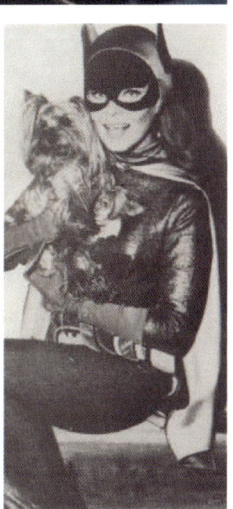

Eartha Kitt as Catwoman.

Doctor Who (and Dalekmania)

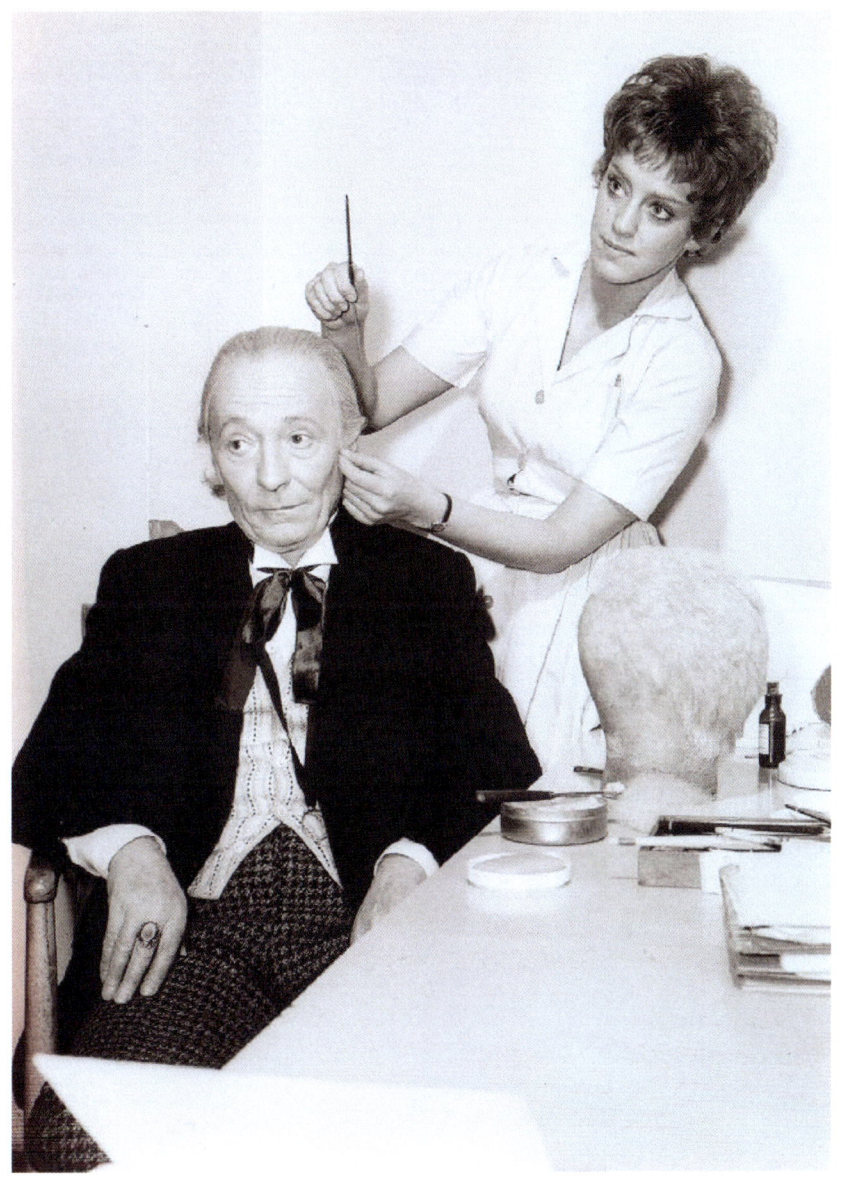

26

"When we take over, the buses will run on time…"

"Sorry, lads, full up"

"Buses are like Dalek stories, there'll be another one along in a minute…"

Doctor Who meets the Eggs-Men.

32

I have no idea what is going on here...

The Doctor looked a bit different on the trading cards...

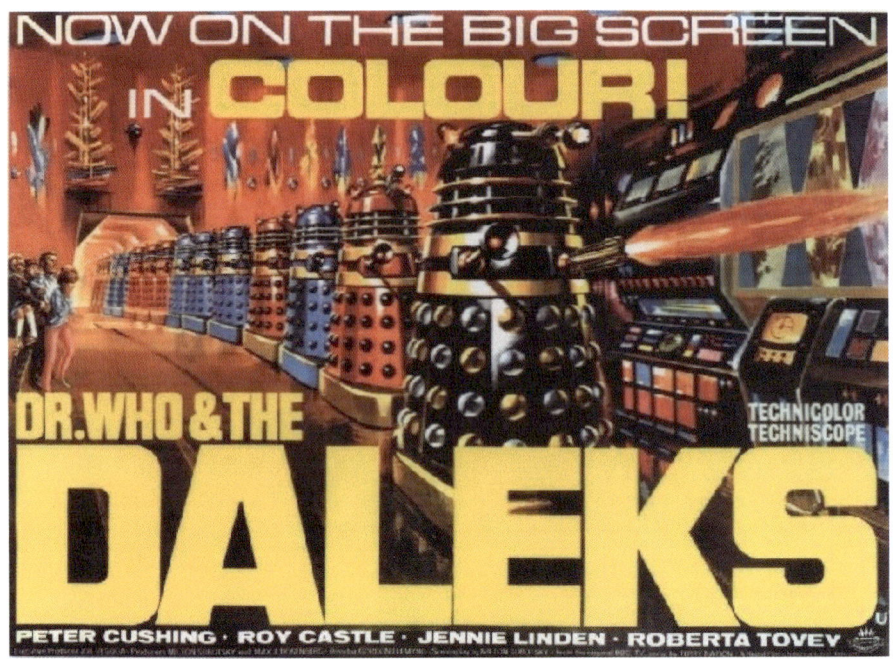

Previous page: Promo materials for the two Doctor Who films made by Amicus, adapting the first two television stories into mediocre but entertaining films. Peter Cushing starred, alongside Roy Castle, Jennie Linden, and Roberta Tovey, joined by Bernard Cribbins for the second. Their main contribution was to take the cliches the television serial had dispensed with, and put them back in! But hell, they were Daleks and they were in colour...

I'd have thought I'd died and gone to heaven if I'd stumbled onto any of these photo shoots when I was ten years old…

37

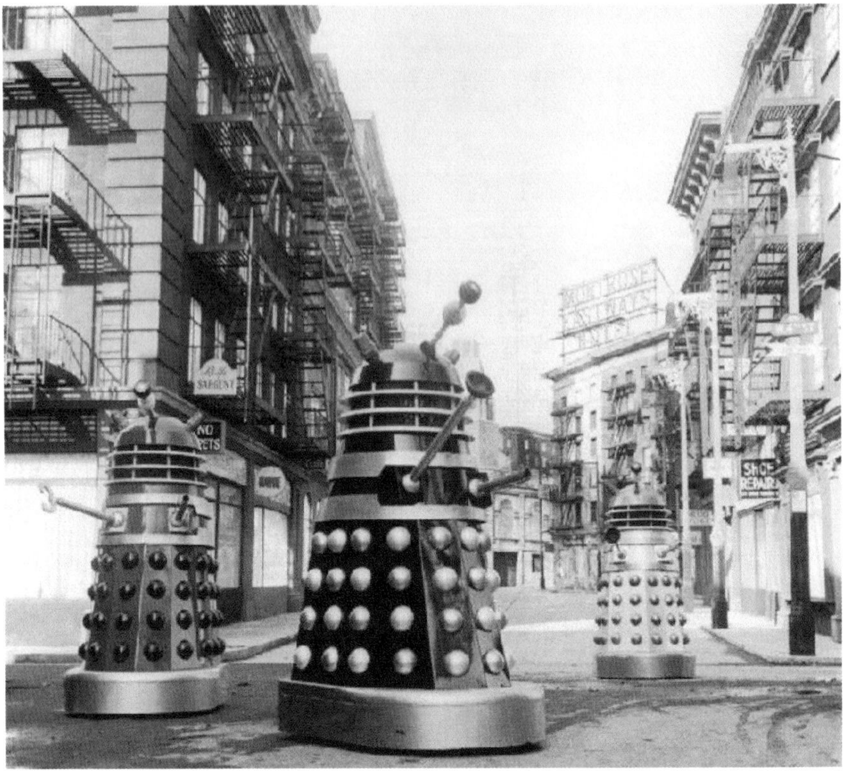
NO PETS

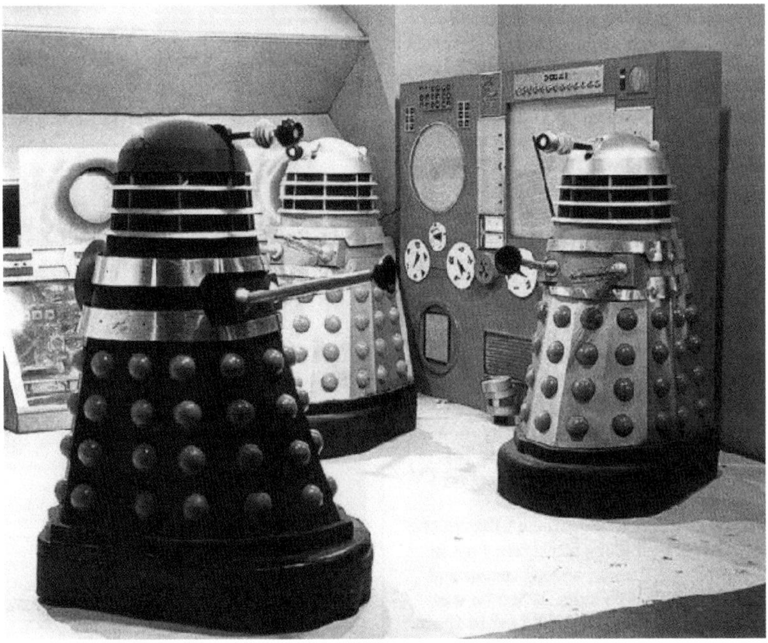

Awkward…

Below: Even a Dalek has to hit his mark…

Defeating the Daleks through the medium of dance…

Two glamour pics…

Left, how to mount a Dalek…

Below, seconds from a fiery death…

It's not only third Doctor Jon Pertwee who looks knackered in this 1970s photo-shoot… even the Daleks are looking a bit threadbare in the shabby Seventies…

The Daleks' 1965 adversaries, the Mechanoids, from the penultimate episodes of "The Chase". Remarkable for the period…

"Are you sure you lost your contact lens in here?"

"Gorra light, love? Ta…"

The ant-like Zarbi and the bee-like Menoptra turned out not to be as popular as hoped, despite getting a comic-strip appearance in TV Comic… It was, however, one of the more surreal experiences of Saturday night TV…

Zarbi, Zanti... and look at the creature bottom left... somebody at the BBC had been watching The Outer Limits on ITV...

Maureen O'Brien and the Koquillion...

New replacement Doctor Who Patrick Troughton (the first) consults the script with a Yeti... ("Yes, but what's my motivation?").

Tea up...

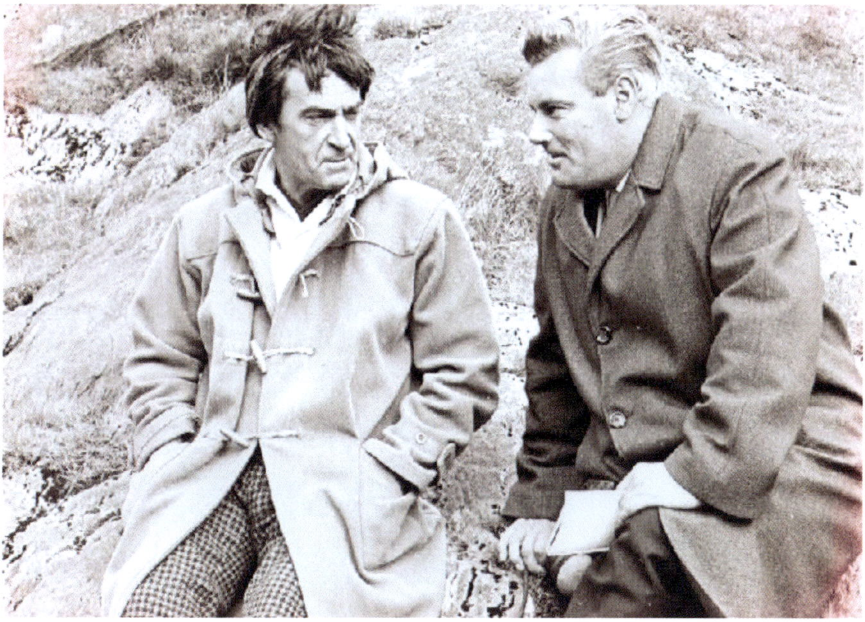

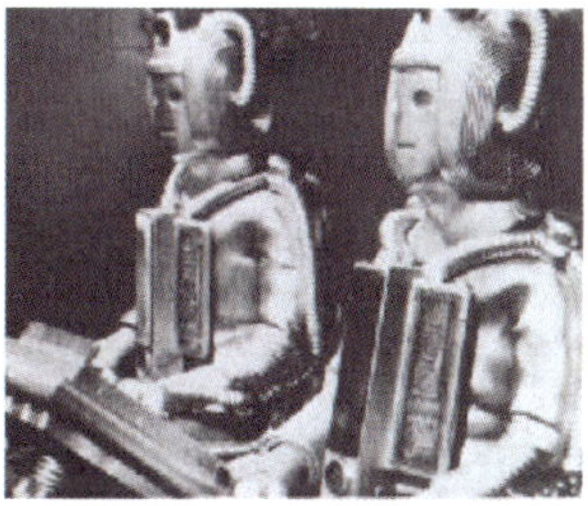

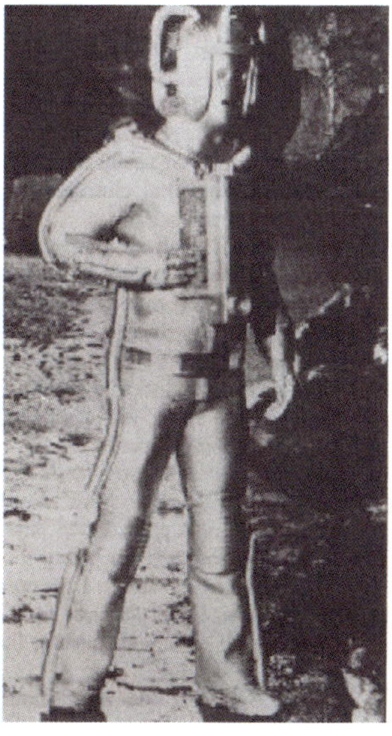

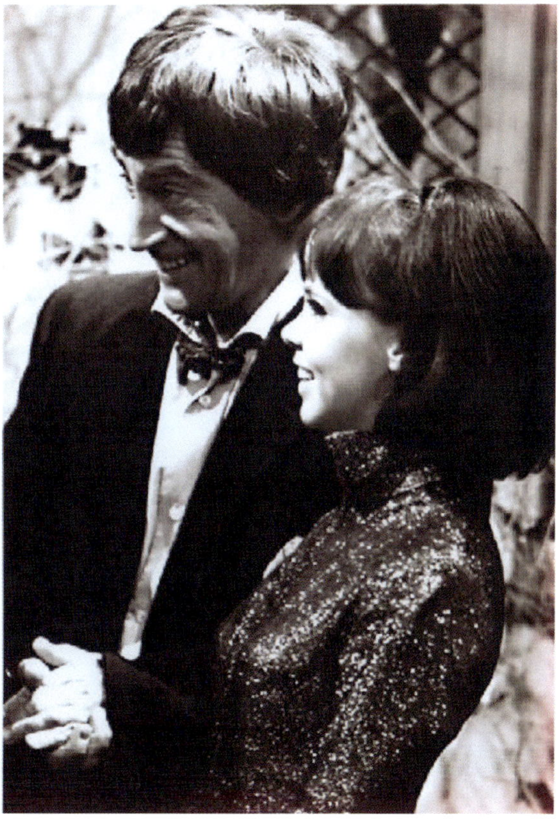

the elvis films

Below, and next page top left: Follow That Dream.

Bottom: Clambake.

Bottom, next page: Blue Hawaii.

52

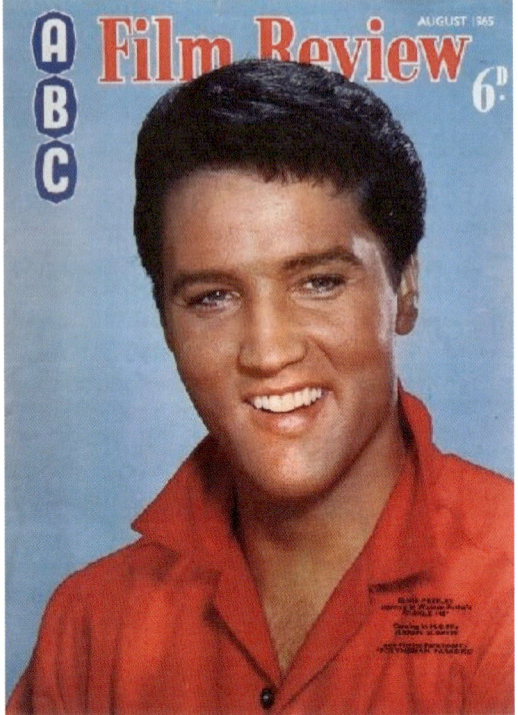

This page: Blue Hawaii.

Top: Soundstage promo shot for Blue Hawaii.

Left and below: Clambake

*Above and next page:
Fun in Acapulco.*

Elvis doesn't seem too impressed to be driving what was also to become the Joker's car in third season Batman in *Easy Come, Easy Go.*

The Batmobile's designer, custom car enthusiast Chuck Barris, was a long-time buddy.

OLE!
ELVIS
ACAPULCO
TECHNICOLOR
AND GIRLS!
NOW
at the
PLAZA
PICCADILLY CIRCUS
and from Dec. 22
AT MOST
ABC
AND OTHER
LEADING CINEMAS
SEE PAGE 54 FOR SPECIAL PRESLEY PASSPORT OFFER
HEAR PRESLEY SING—
TECHNICOLOR
ELVIS
PRESLEY
"FUN IN ACAPULC
A HAL WALLIS Product

JANUARY 1964
Price in Australia and New Zealand 2/-
1/6
OPLAY
"FUN IN ACAPULCO"

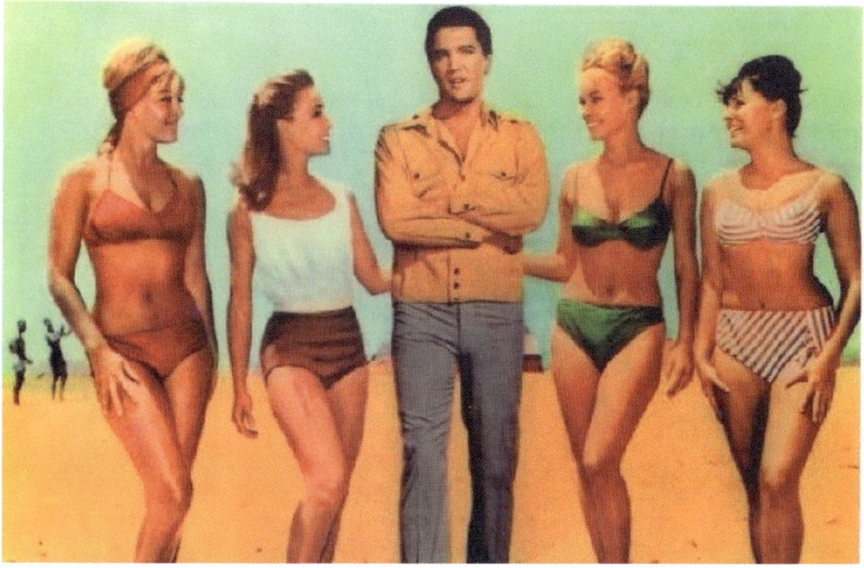

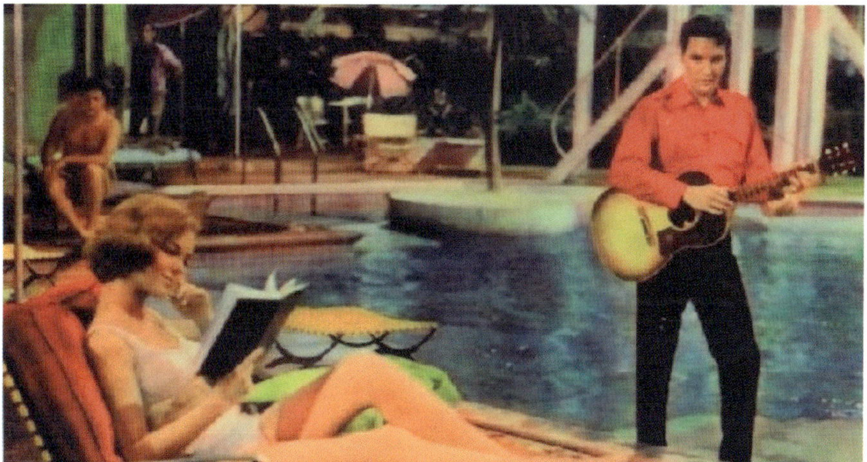

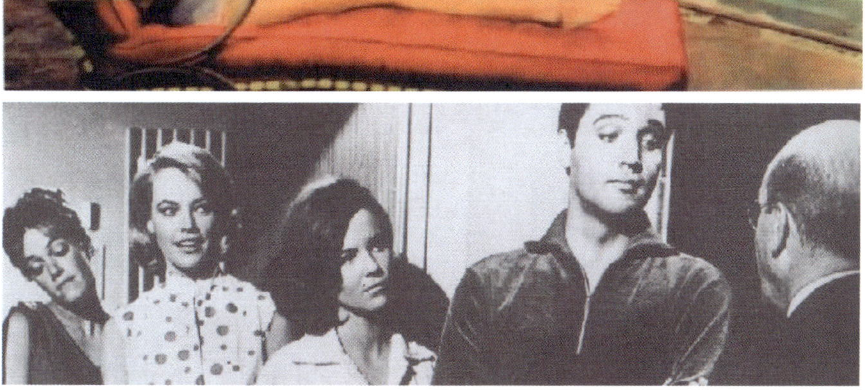

The Swingin'-est ELVIS!
+
GIRLS (GIRLS, GIRLS)
+
SONGS (LOTS OF THEM)
WHO COULD ASK FOR ANYTHING MORE?
MATINEE SHOWING ONLY!
ELVIS PRESLEY
HAL WALLIS' PRODUCTION
"GIRLS! GIRLS! GIRLS!"
13 OF THE COOLEST SONGS IN RCA'S FABULOUS "GIRLS! GIRLS! GIRLS!" ALBUM!
TECHNICOLOR
STELLA STEVENS · JEREMY SLATE · LAUREL GOODWIN

59

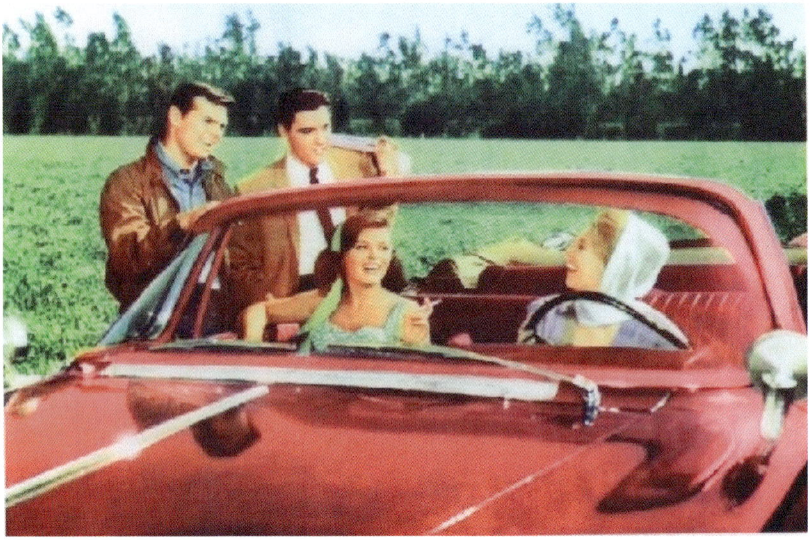

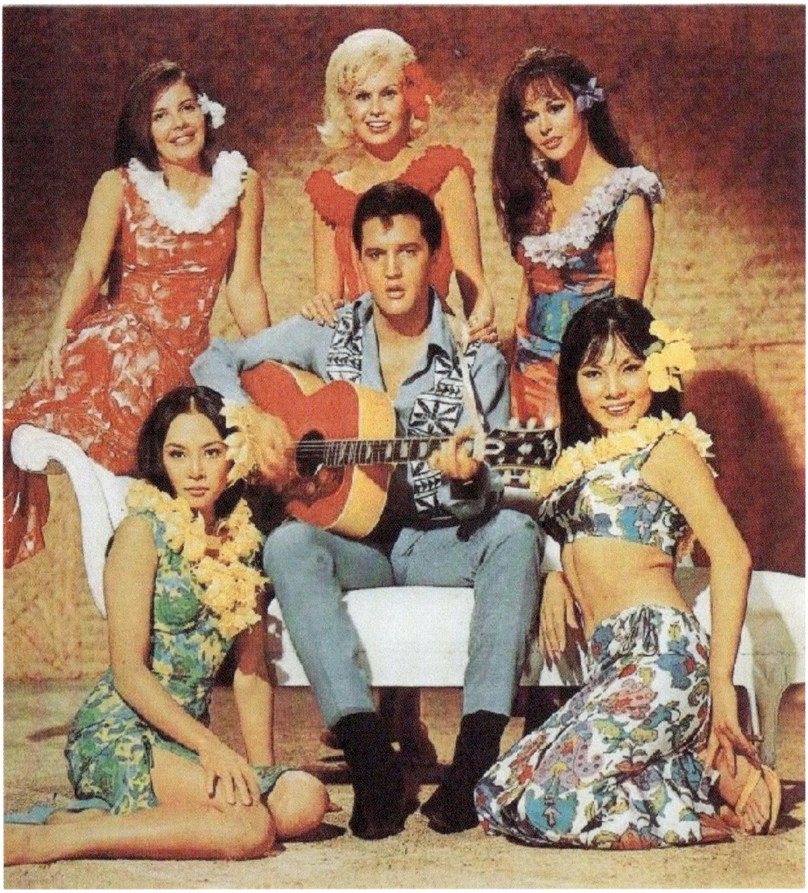

Page 57: Girl Happy.

Pages. 58 and 59:
Girls! Girls! Girls!

Top Left, page 60:
It Happened At the
World's Fair.

Lower left and this page:
Paradise Hawaiian Style.

Next page: Speedway and
below, Tickle Me.

61

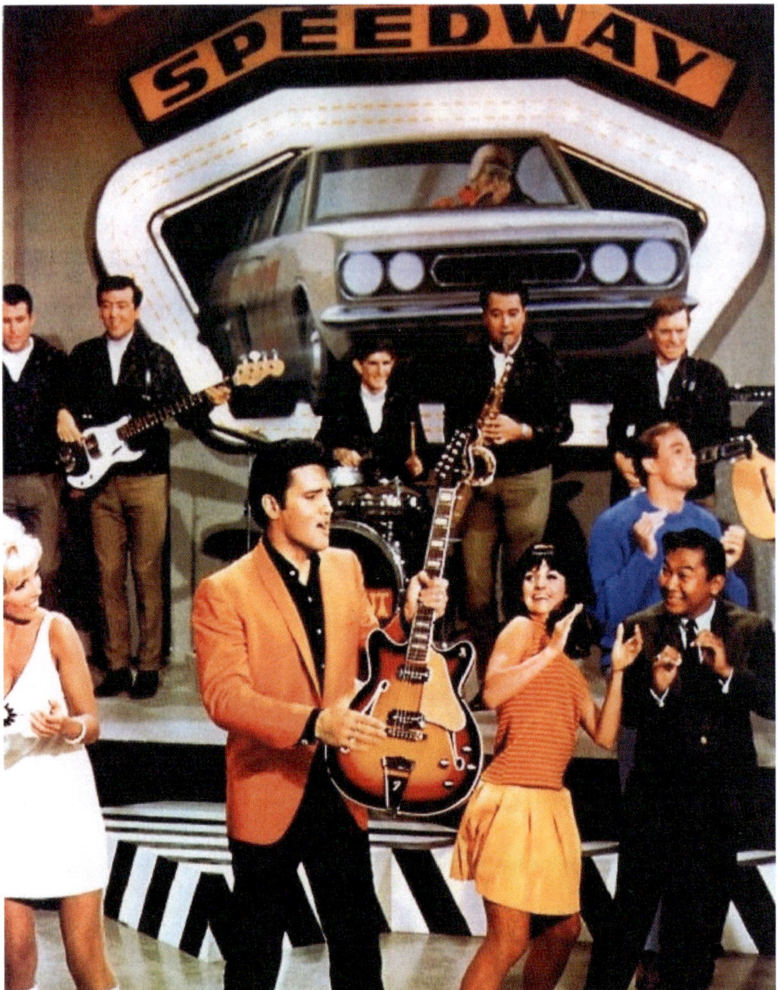
SPEEDWAY

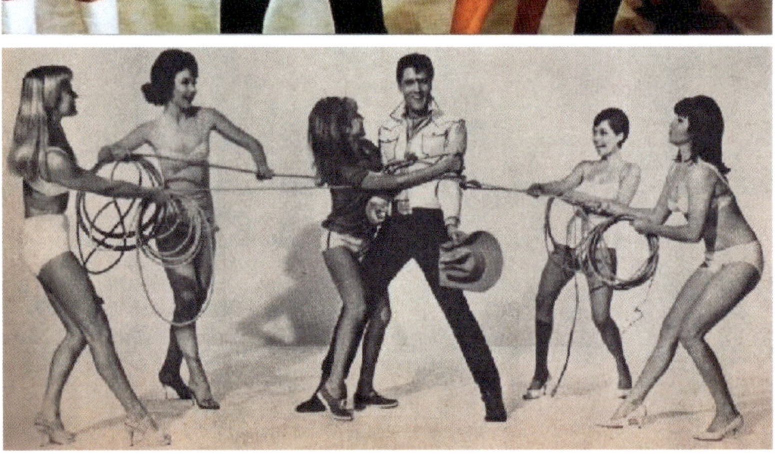

Top: Spinout.

Left and below: Viva Las Vegas.

This page and next pages: Viva Las Vegas

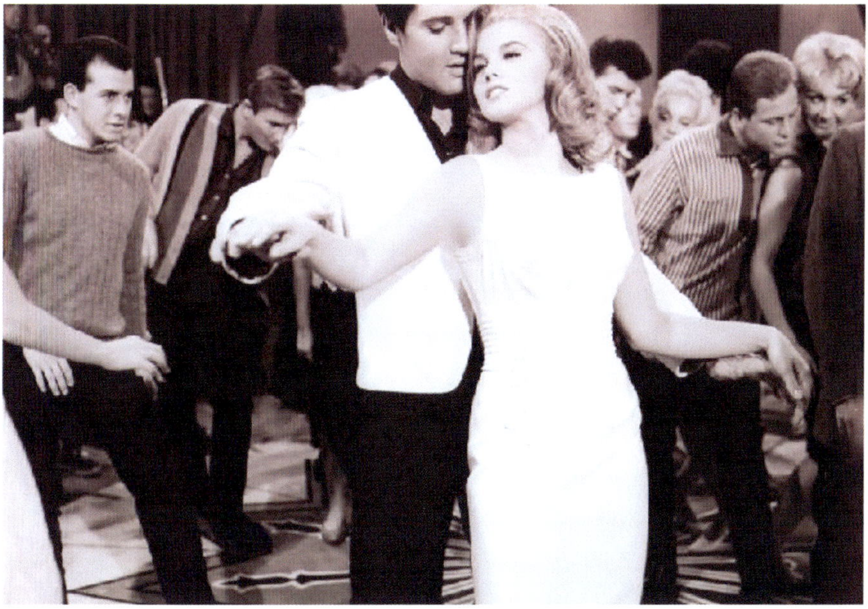

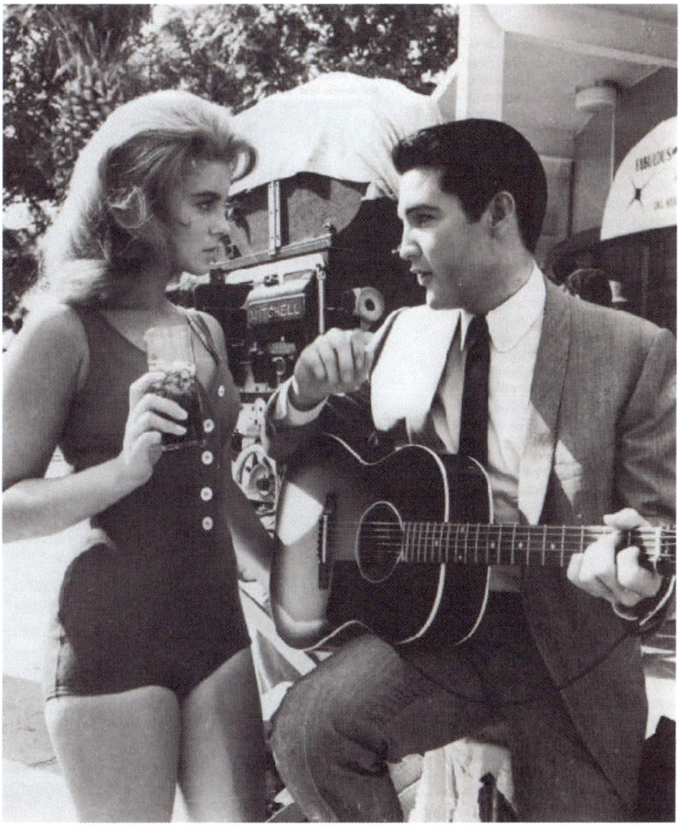

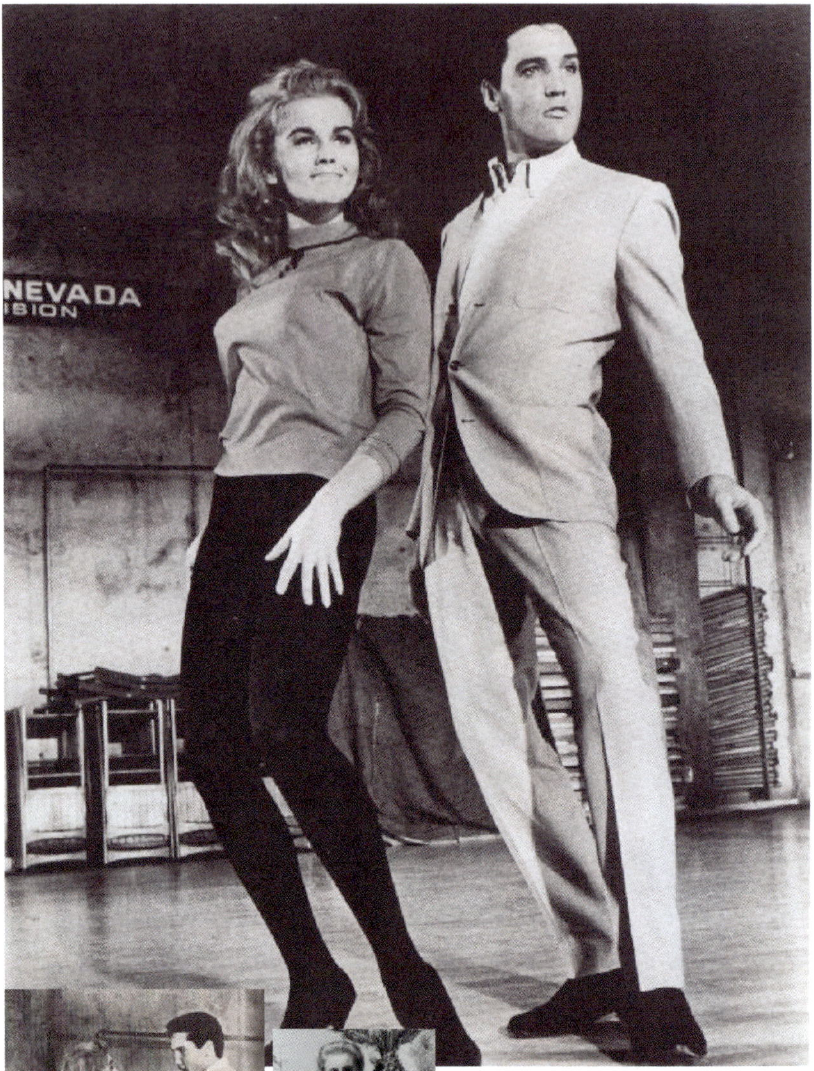
NEVADA
ISION

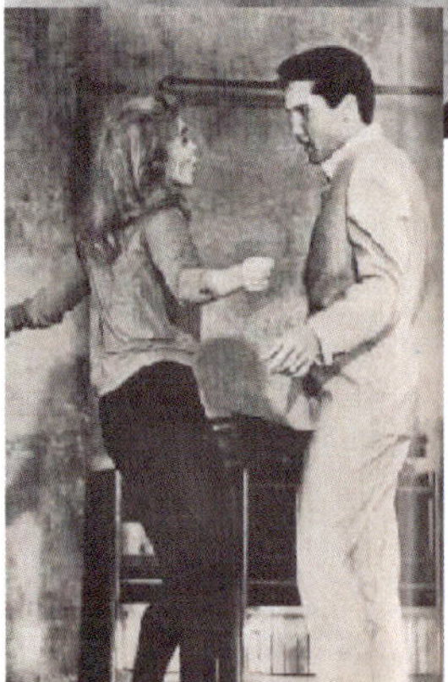

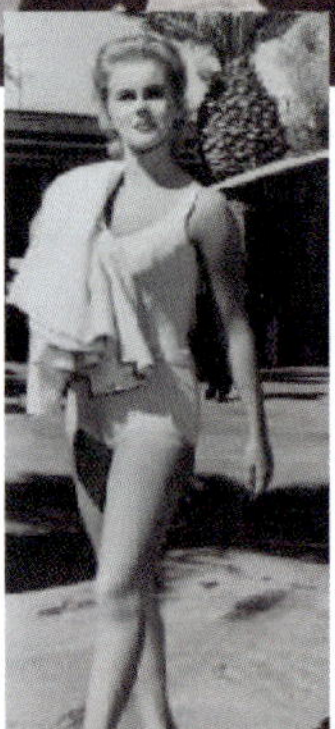

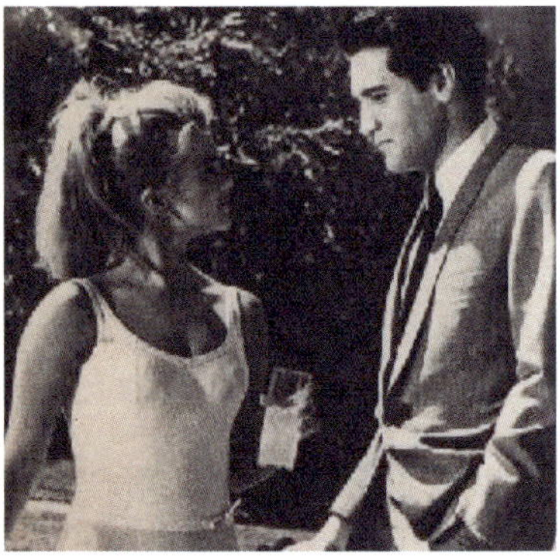

Gerry Anderson and Super-Marionation

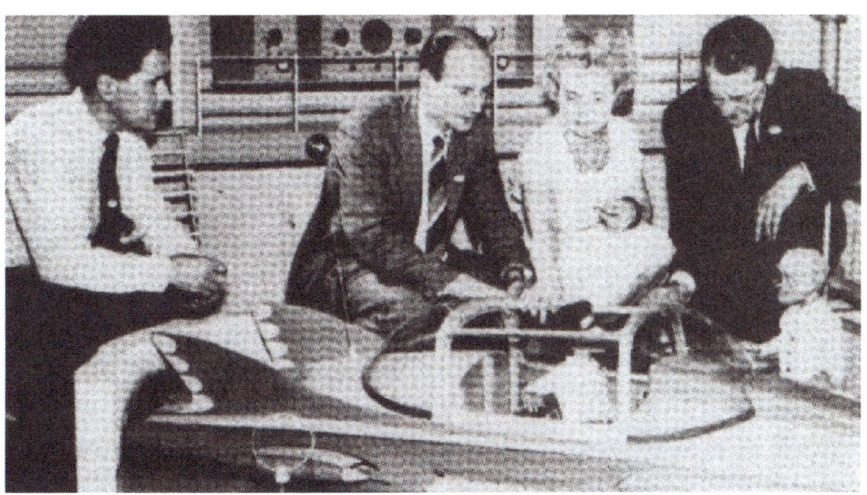

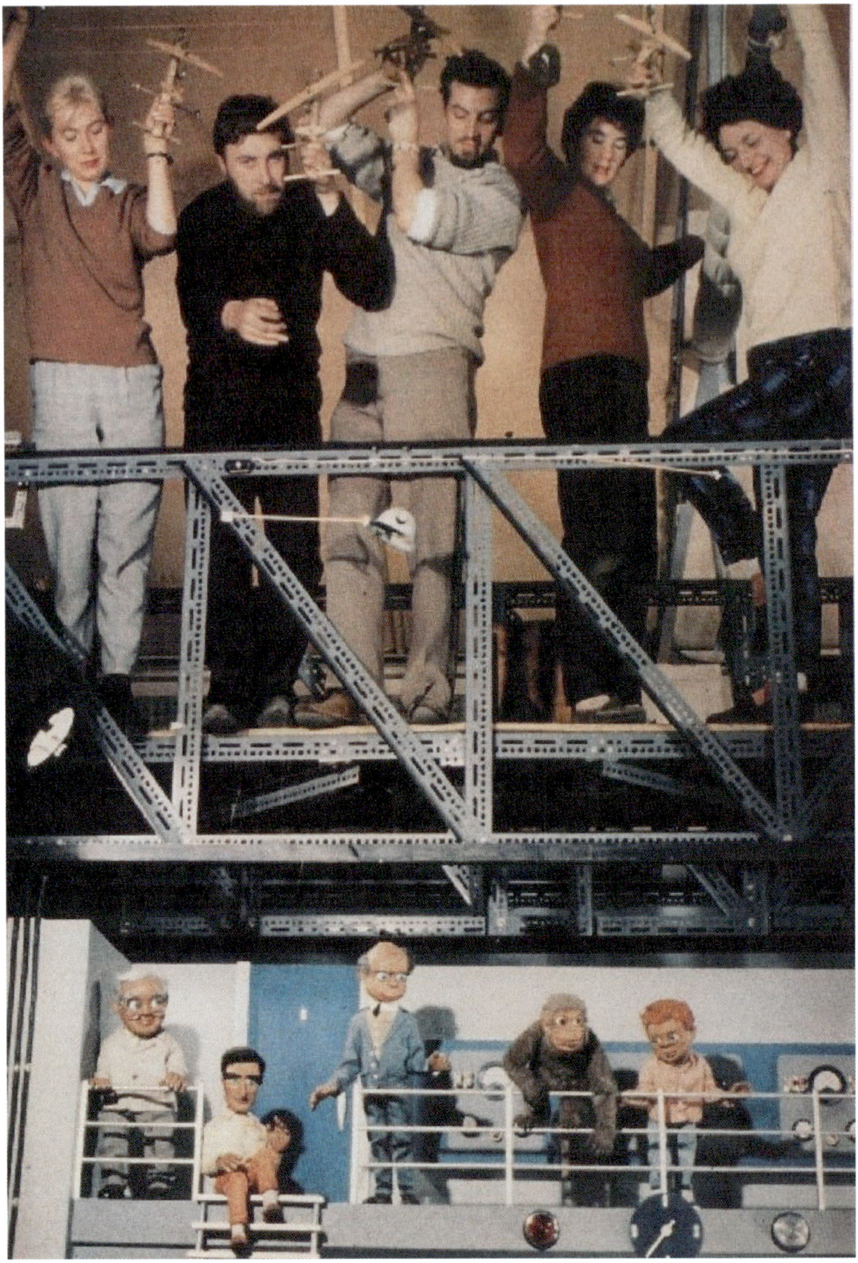

SUPERCAR
THE CHILDREN'S TELEVISION FAVOURITE
ANNUAL
SUPERCAR
INTRODUCING
SUPER-R
SUPER-R
SUPER-R

SUPERCAR
ANNUAL
SUPERCAR
TELEVISION'S TOP FAVOURITE!

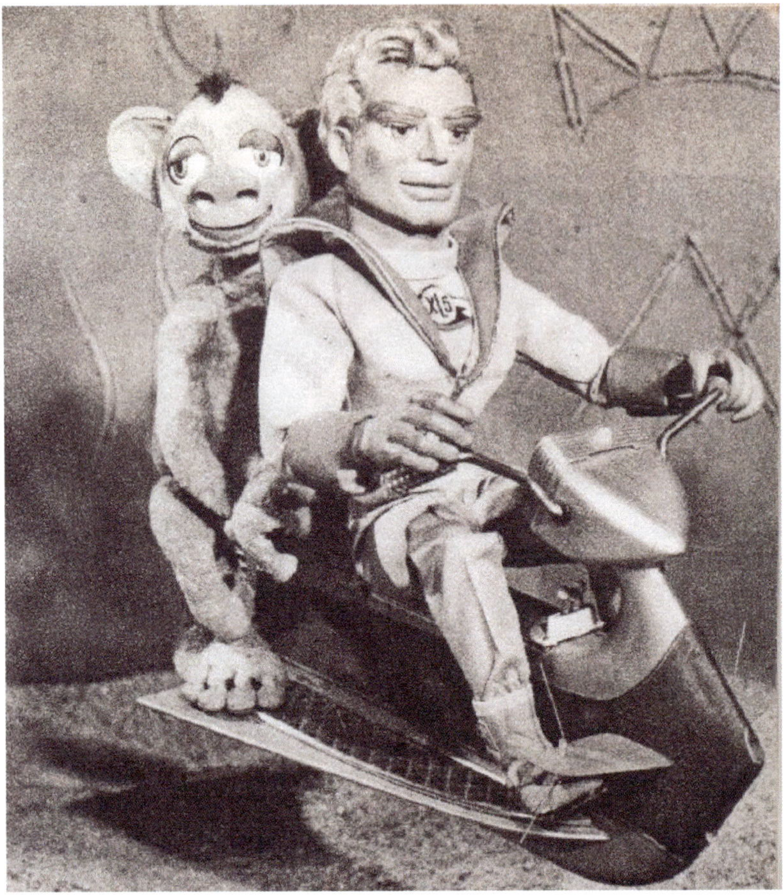

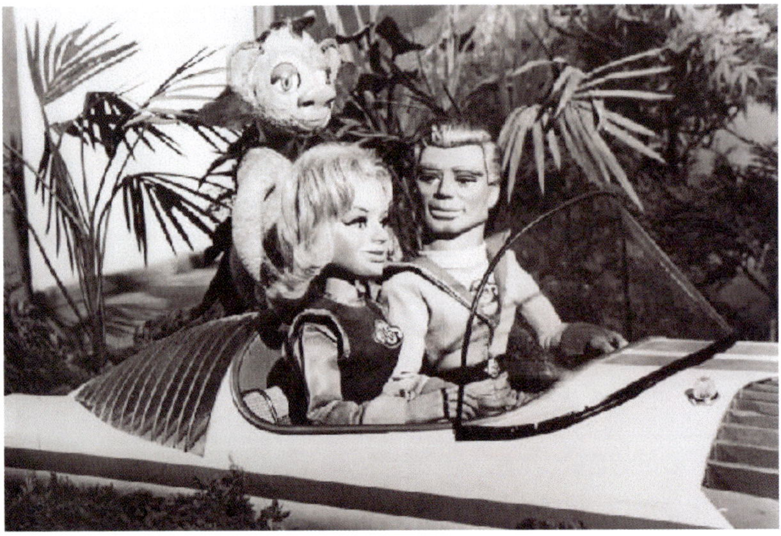

71

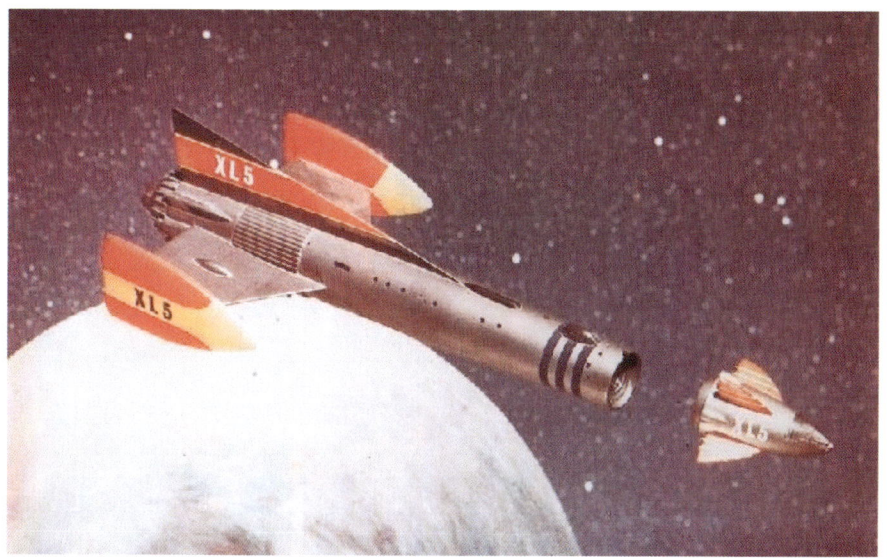

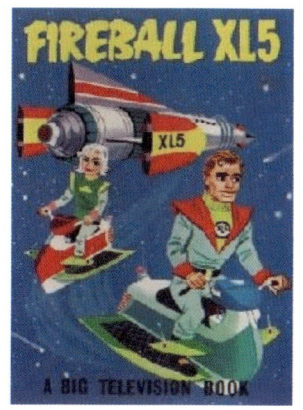

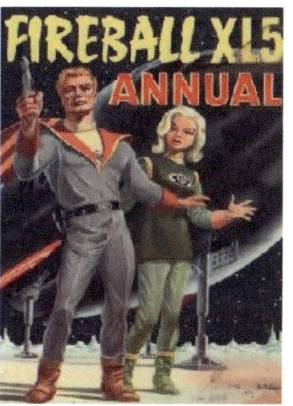

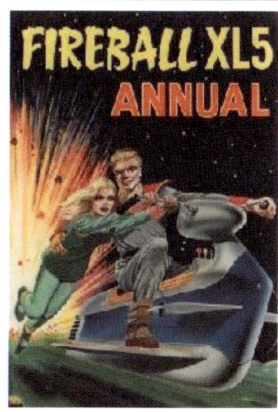

In emergencies, Stingray's Marineville sinks to safety underground...

72

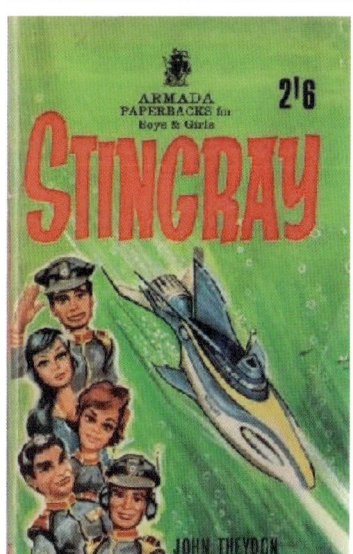

Above and next page: recurring bad guy Titan in his elaborate undersea palace…

73

In the first episode, hero Troy Tempest rescues mute mermaid Marina from undersea despot Titan, the series' resident bad guy.

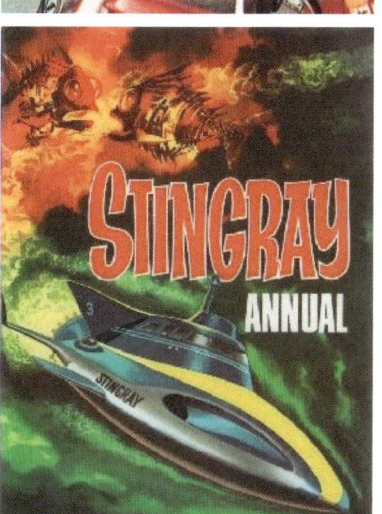

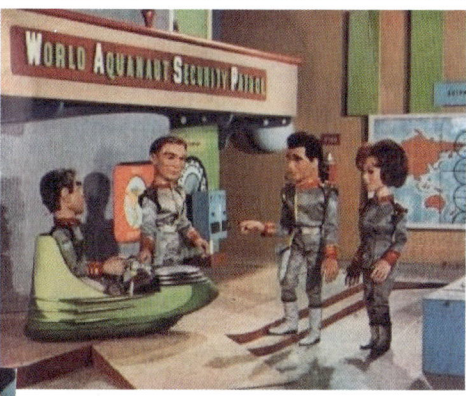

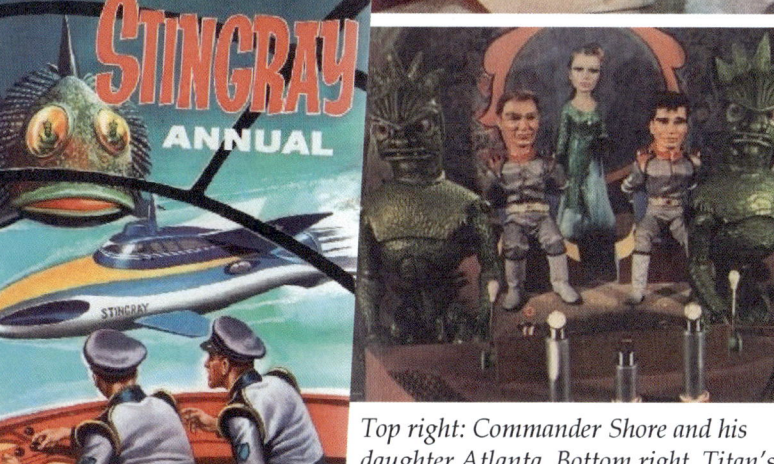

Top right: Commander Shore and his daughter Atlanta. Bottom right, Titan's disposable stooges, the Aquaphibians.

The series' attention to the smallest detail gave it an extraordinary sophistication for a childrens' puppet production, with miniature ornaments, condiments, and possessions for interiors and credible, futuristic surroundings that looked lived in…

The characters sat down to meals, drove vehicles, and enjoyed recreational pleasures that included wine, good food, books, and vinyl record collections!

GIRL OF THE SEA

Marina

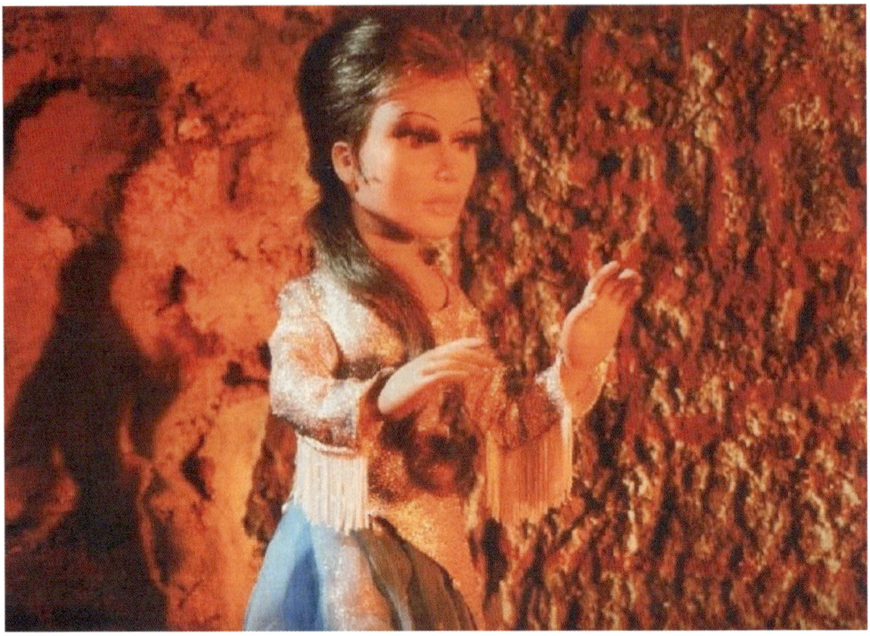

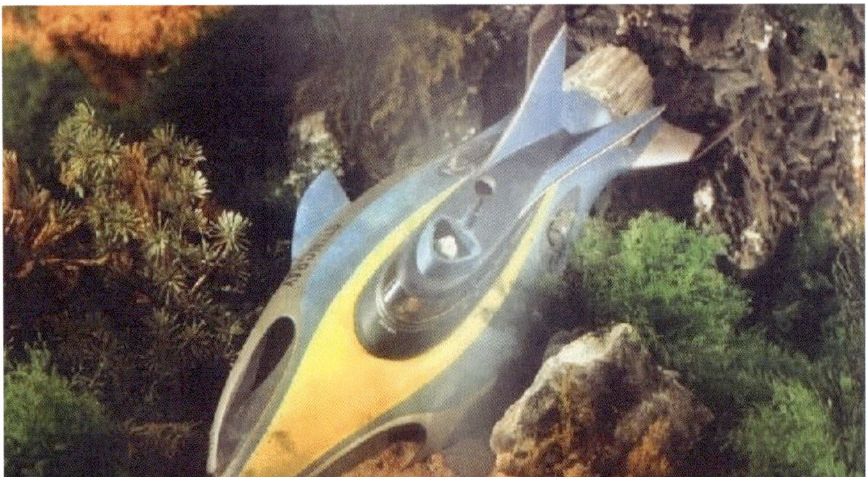

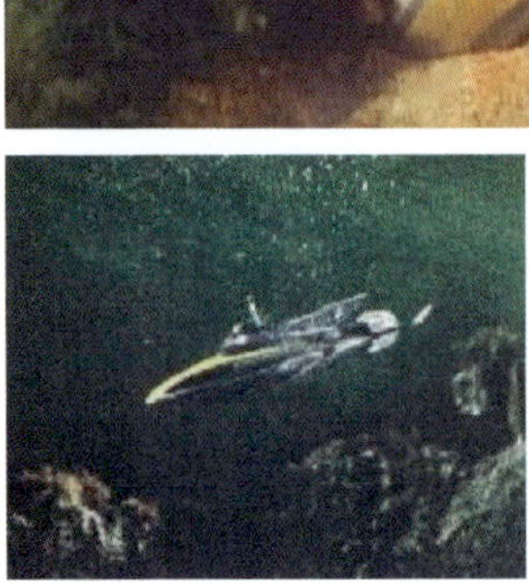

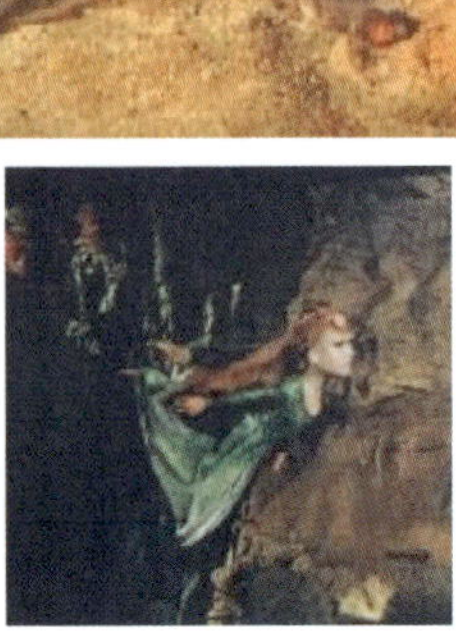

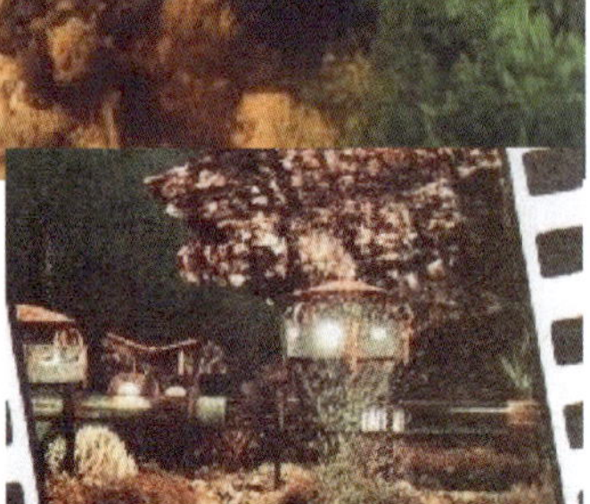

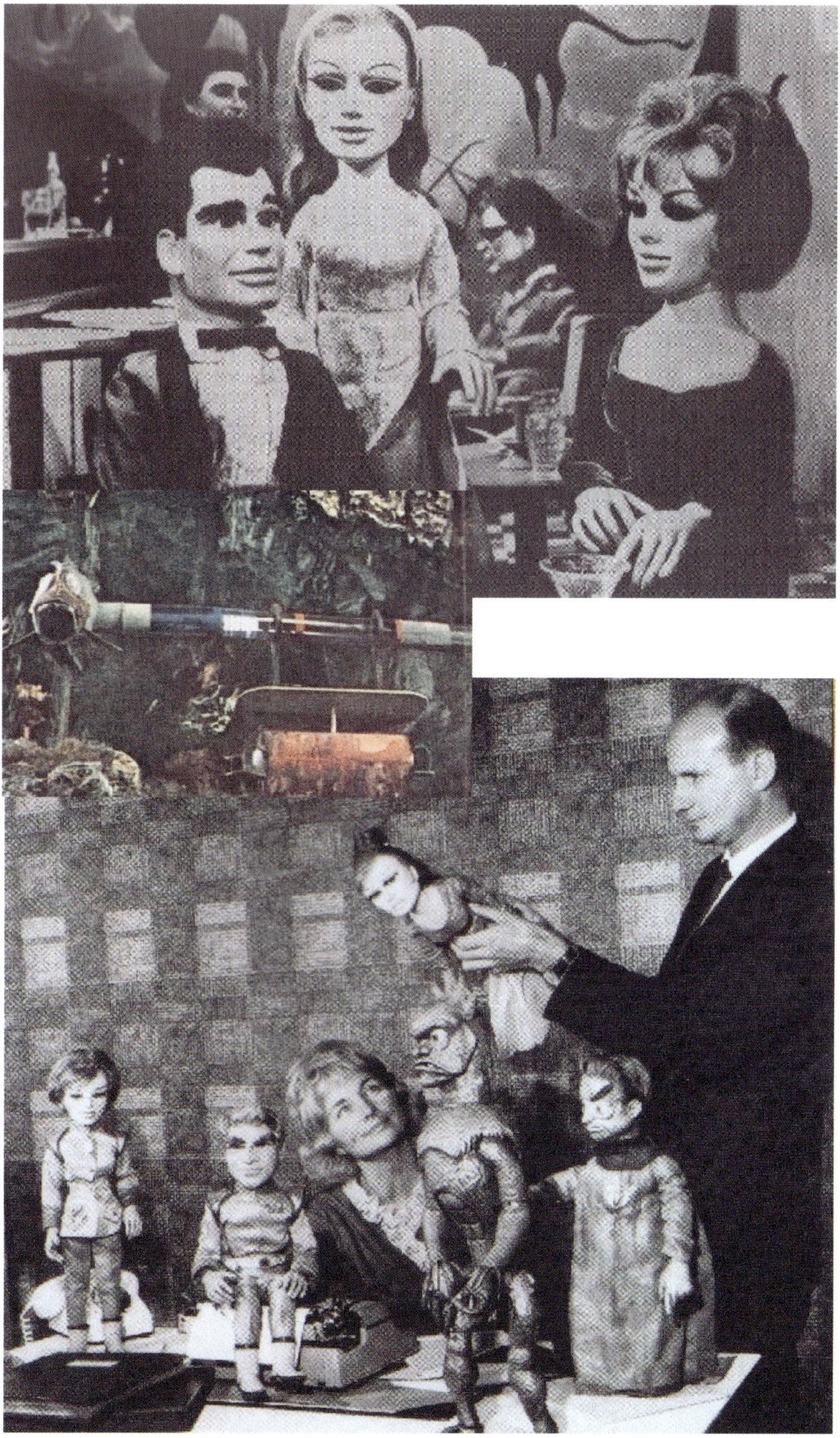

COUNT DOWN BEGINS
Space Monitor John Tracy is Ready
THUNDERBIRDS
ARE COMING
5

THUNDERBIRDS ARE COMING !
4
3

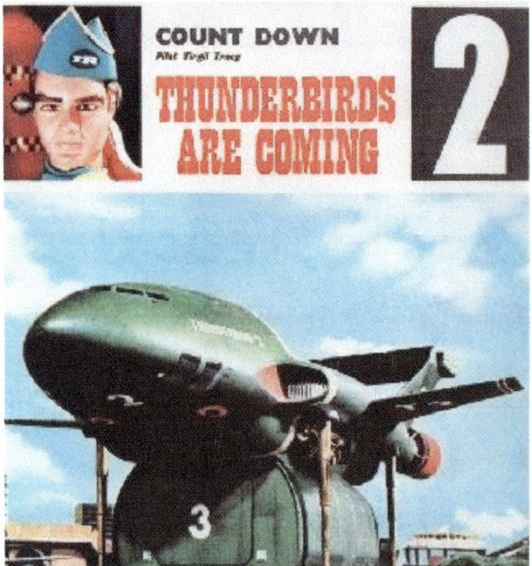
COUNT DOWN
THUNDERBIRDS
ARE COMING
2

THEIR FIRST BIG SCREEN ADVENTURE IN COLOUR!
THUNDERBIRDS
ARE
GO

1
COUNT DOWN
Final Checks
All systems are
Go for
THUNDERBIRDS

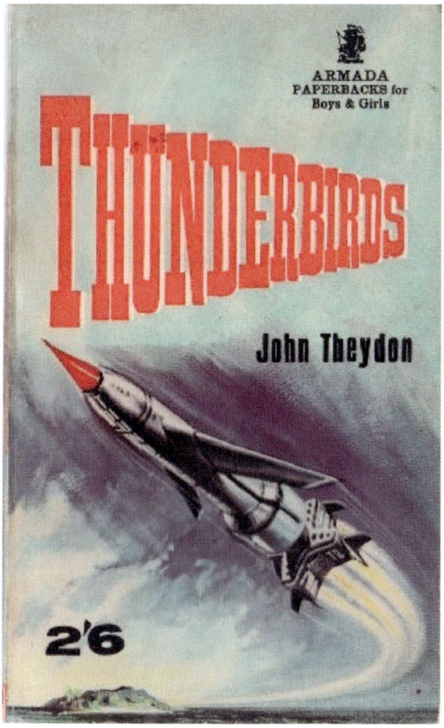
ARMADA
PAPERBACKS for
Boys & Girls
THUNDERBIRDS
John Theydon
2'6

ARMADA
PAPERBACKS for
Boys & Girls
CALLING
THUNDERBIRDS
John Theydon
2/6

THUNDERBIRD 2

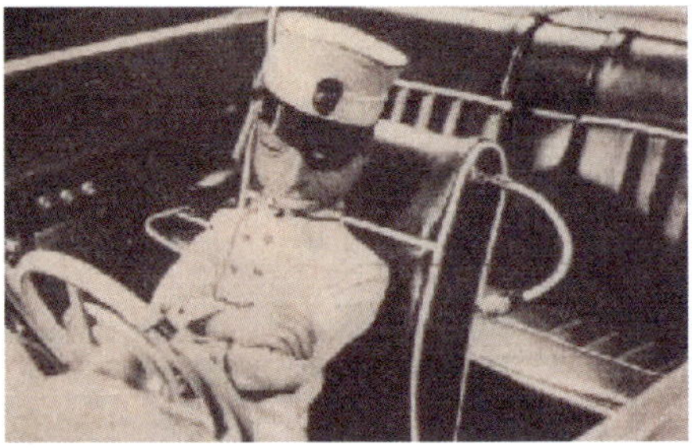

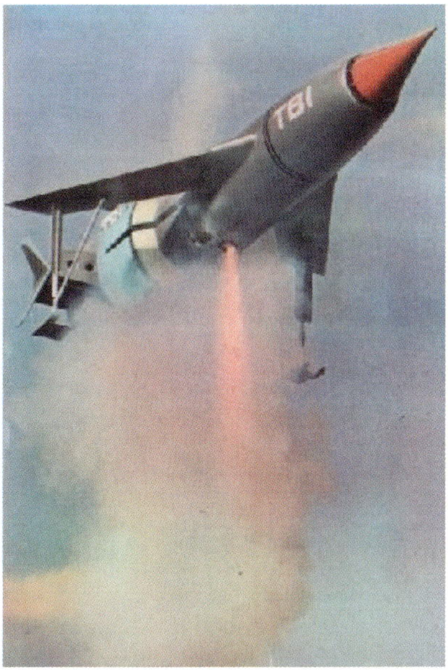
TB1

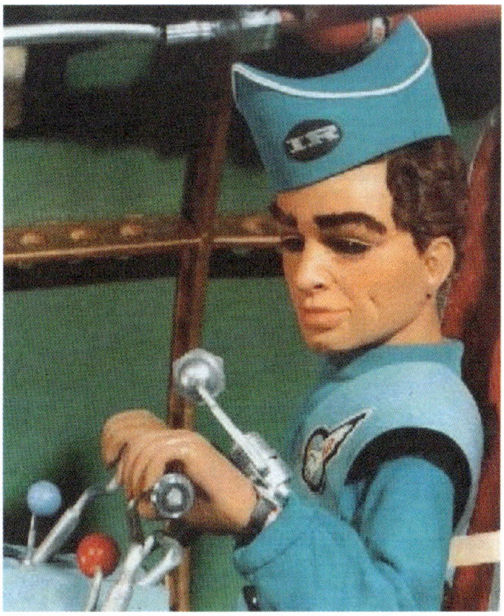
IR

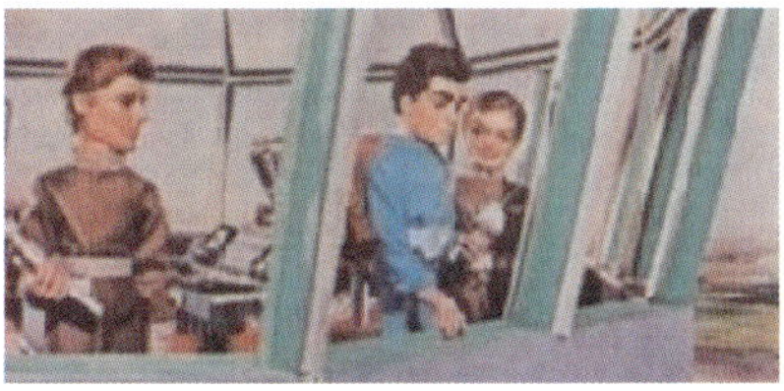

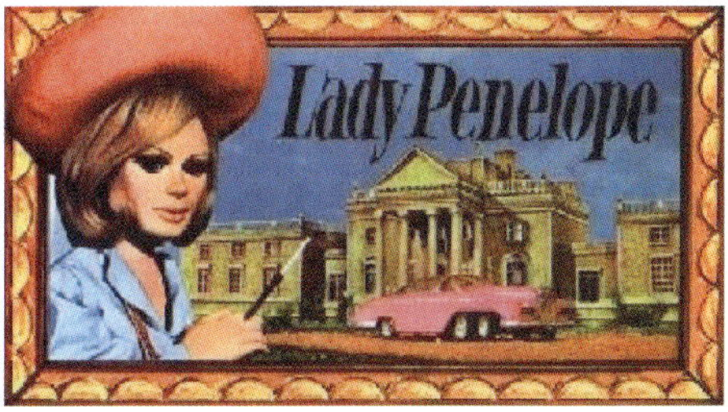
Lady Penelope

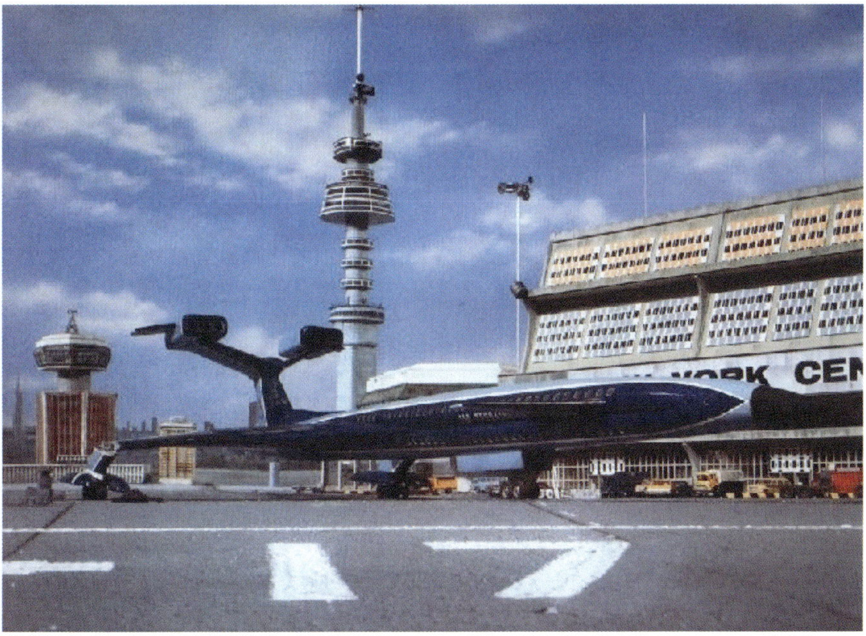

Waddington's
THUNDERBIRDS
Vari-Piece JIG-SAW
TB-1
GERRY ANDERSON'S
THUNDERBIRDS
FILMED IN
1965 A P FILMS LTD., & I T C LTD.
FULLY INTERLOCKING · SIZE 10½" x 13" · OVER 250 PIECES

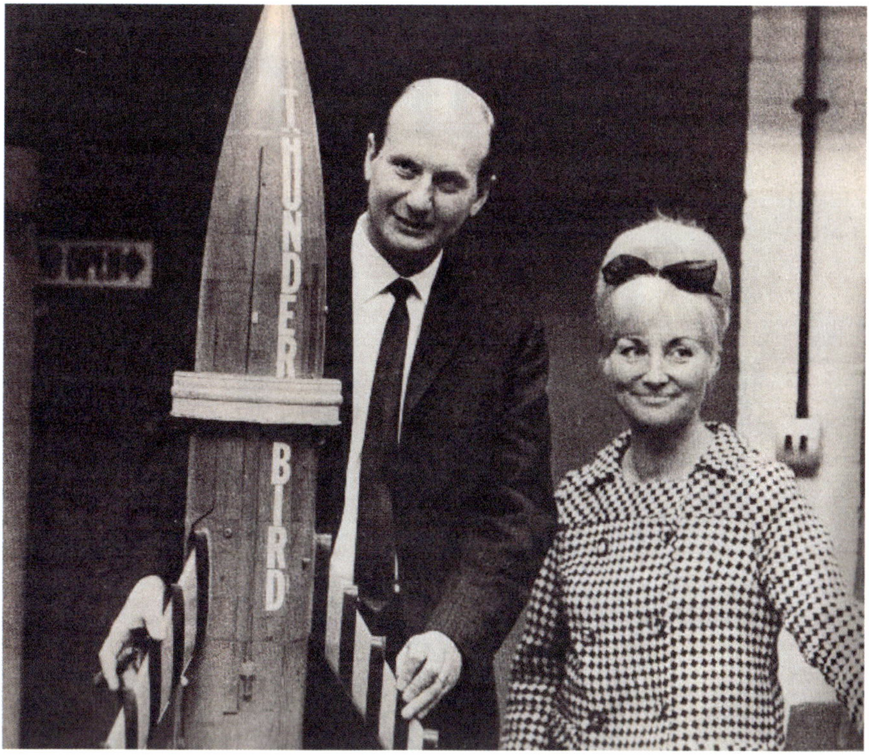
THUNDER
BIRD

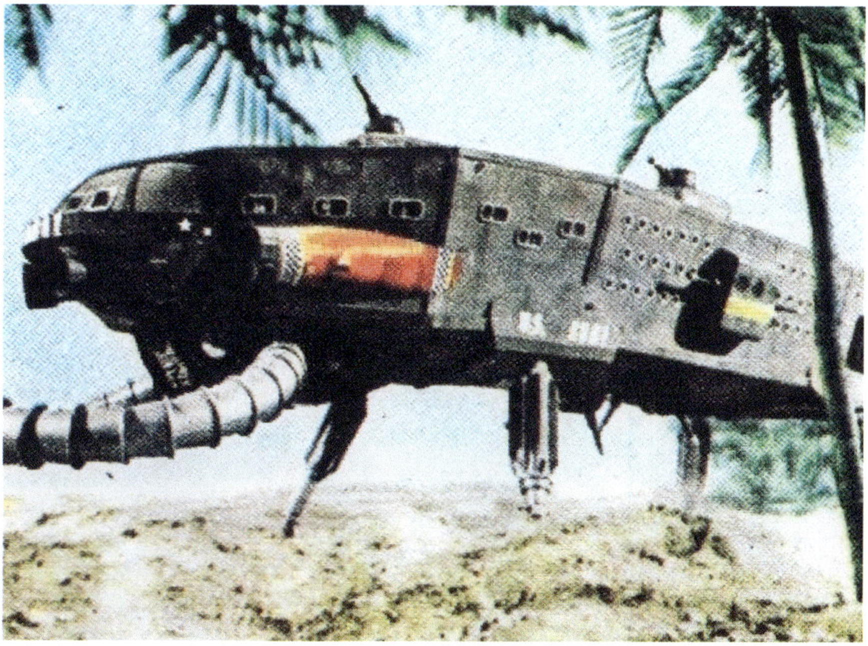

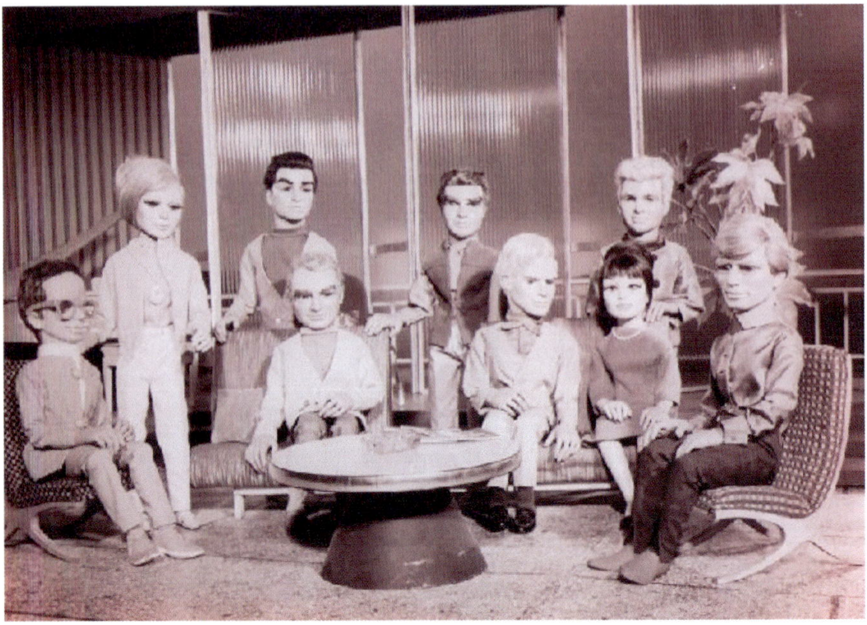

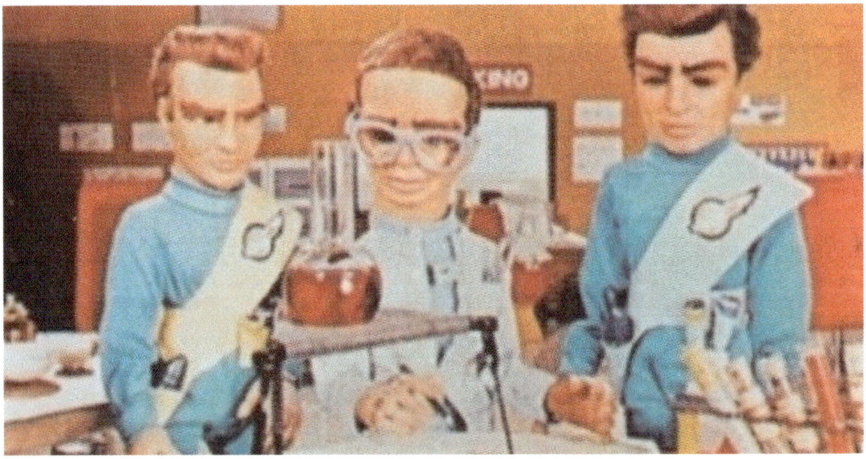

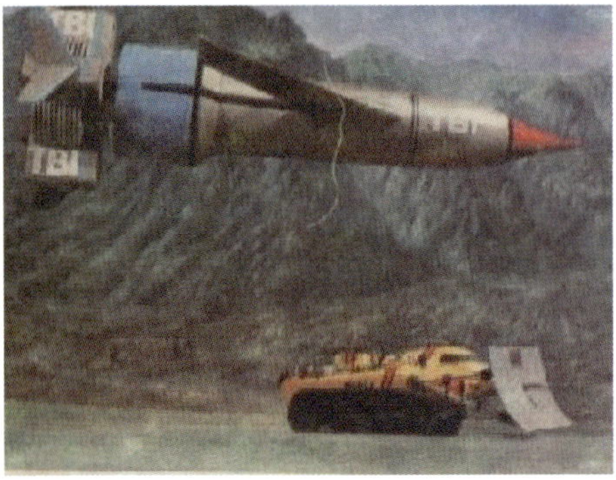

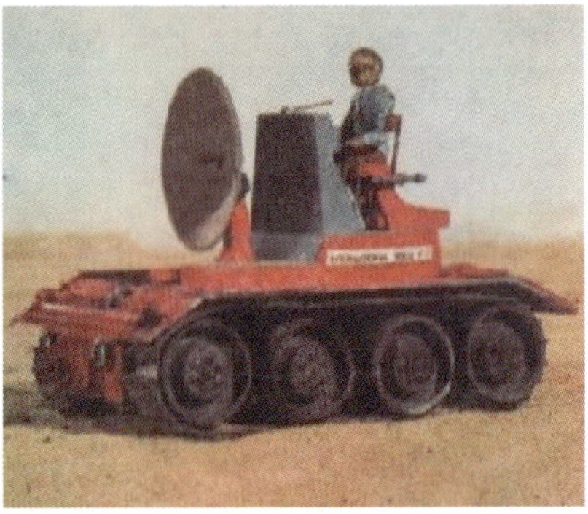

Special effects wizard Derek Meddings (left) came on board during production of Supercar, *and went on to do effects for the Bond movies.*

Here, he's working on Captain Scarlet and the Mysterons.

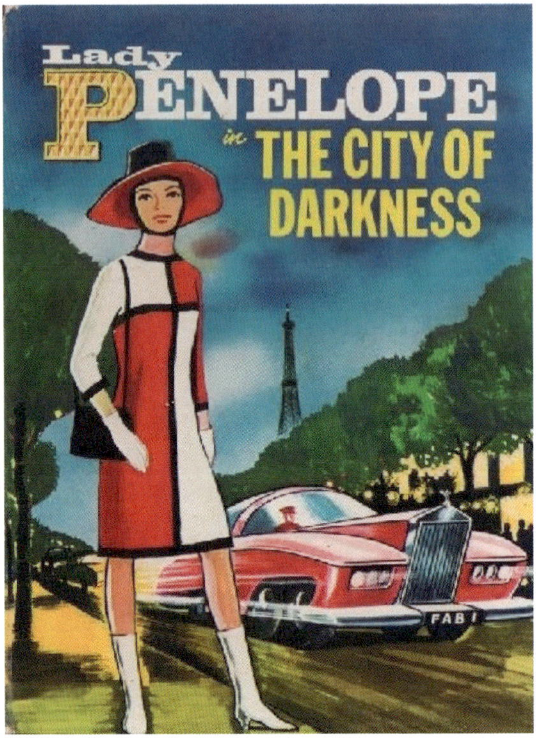
Lady
PENELOPE
in
THE CITY OF
DARKNESS
FAB 1

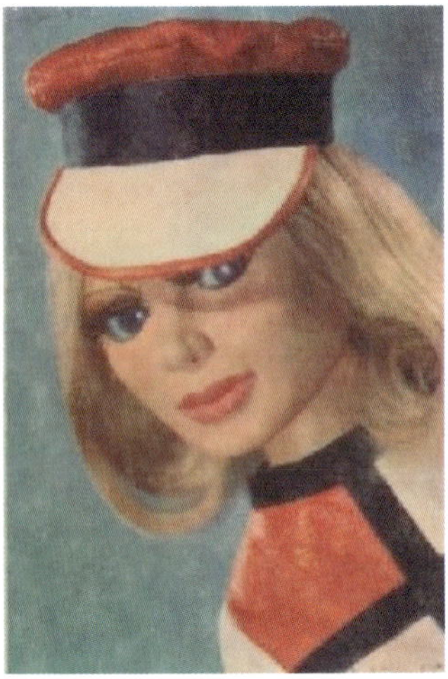

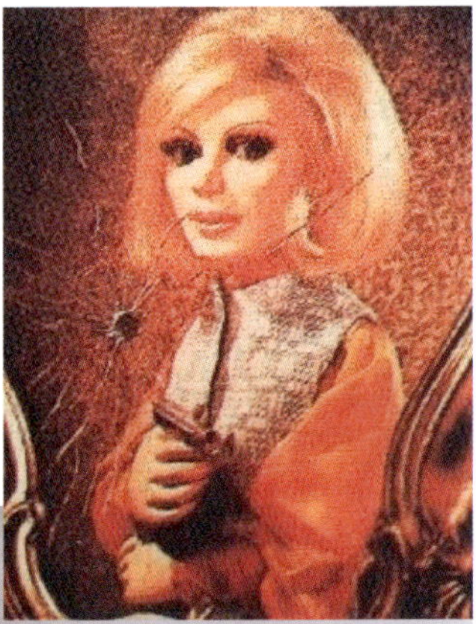

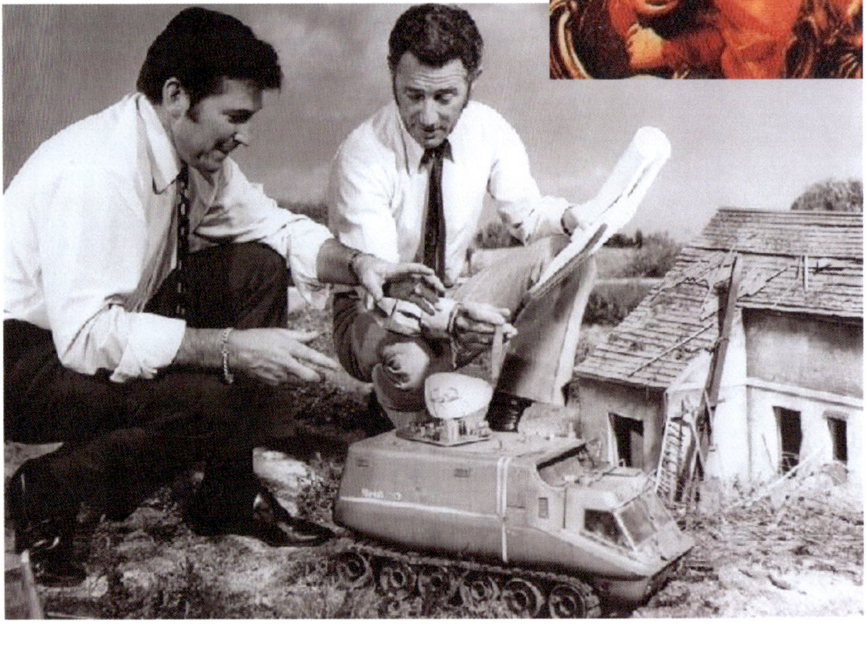

Irwin Allen at 20th Century Fox

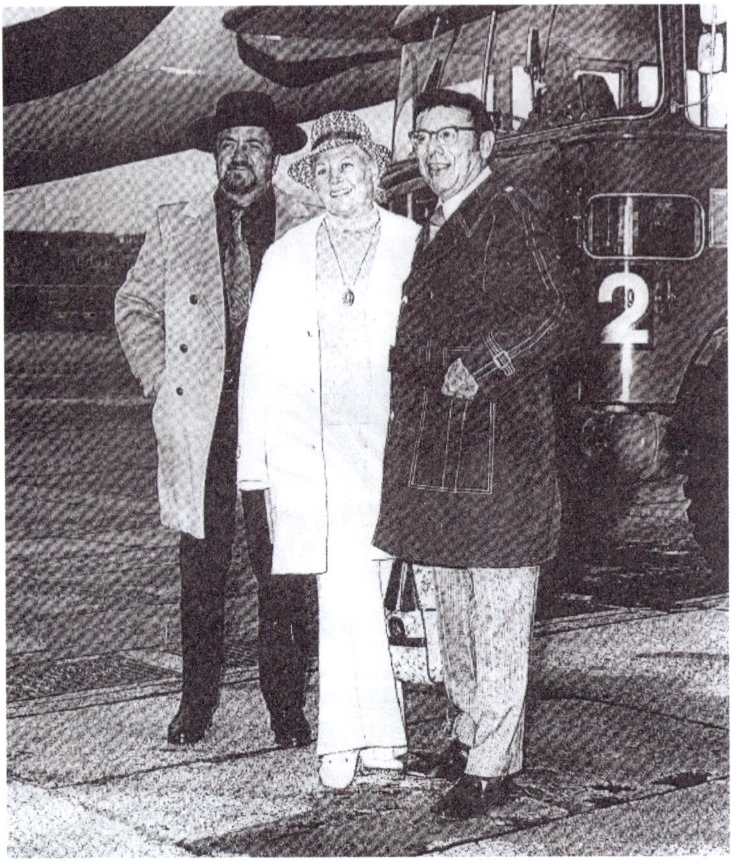
2

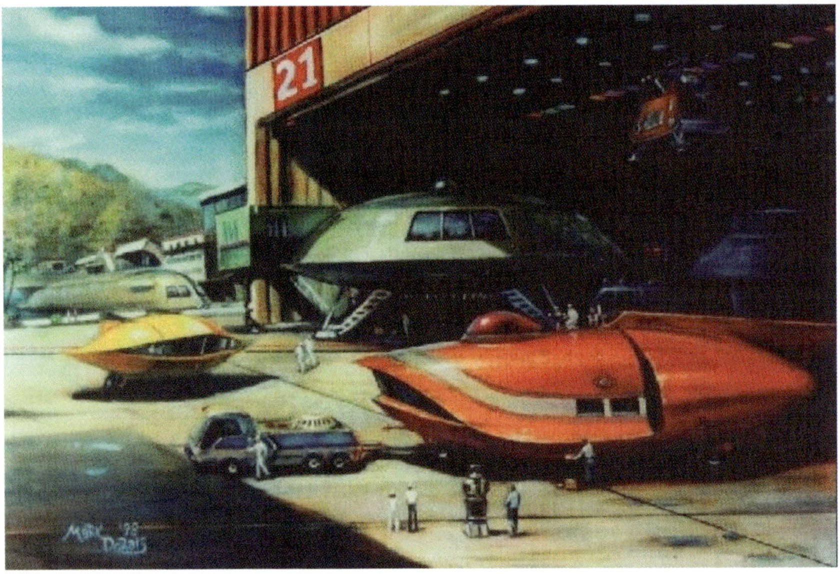
21

91

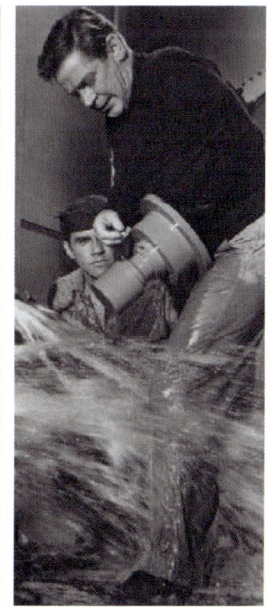

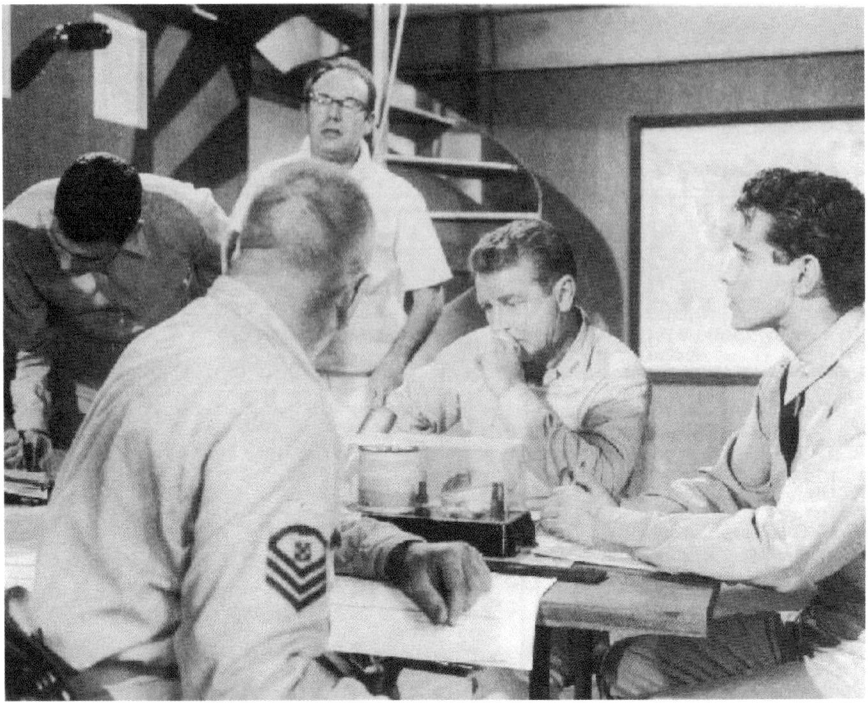

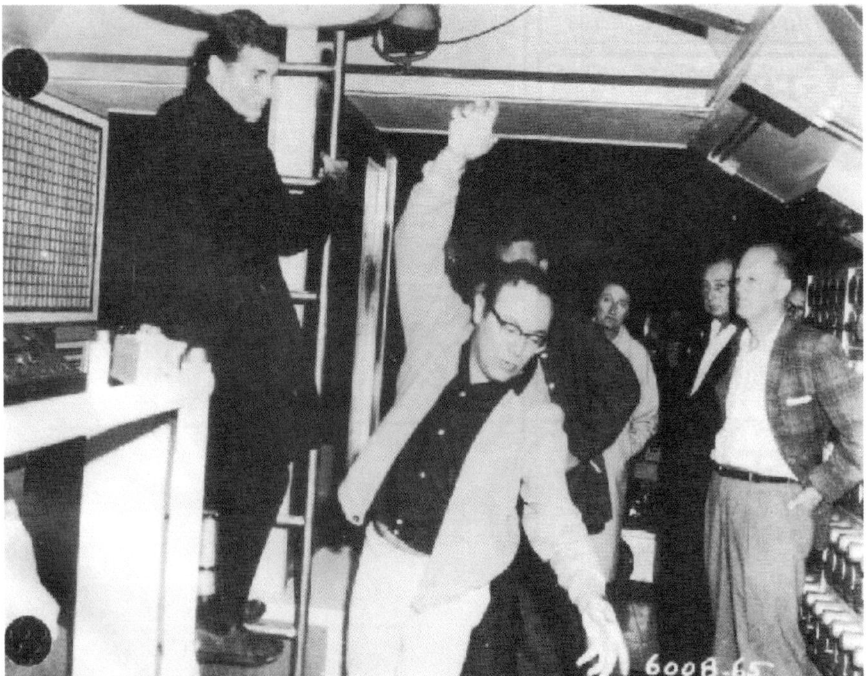
600B-65

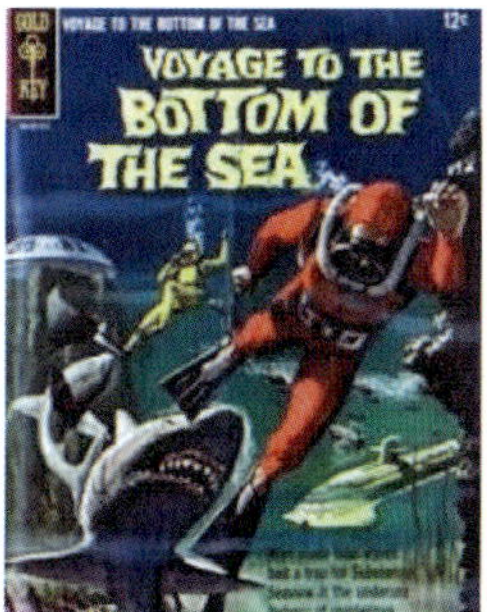
GOLD KEY
VOYAGE TO THE BOTTOM OF THE SEA
12¢
VOYAGE TO THE BOTTOM OF THE SEA
DOCTOR GAMMA

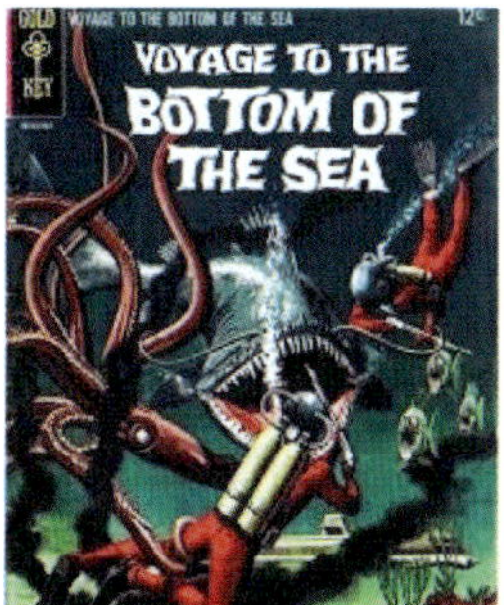
GOLD KEY
VOYAGE TO THE BOTTOM OF THE SEA
12¢
VOYAGE TO THE BOTTOM OF THE SEA
A mysterious fluid from the center of the earth threatens to turn all ocean life into monsters!

VOYAGE TO THE BOTTOM OF THE SEA

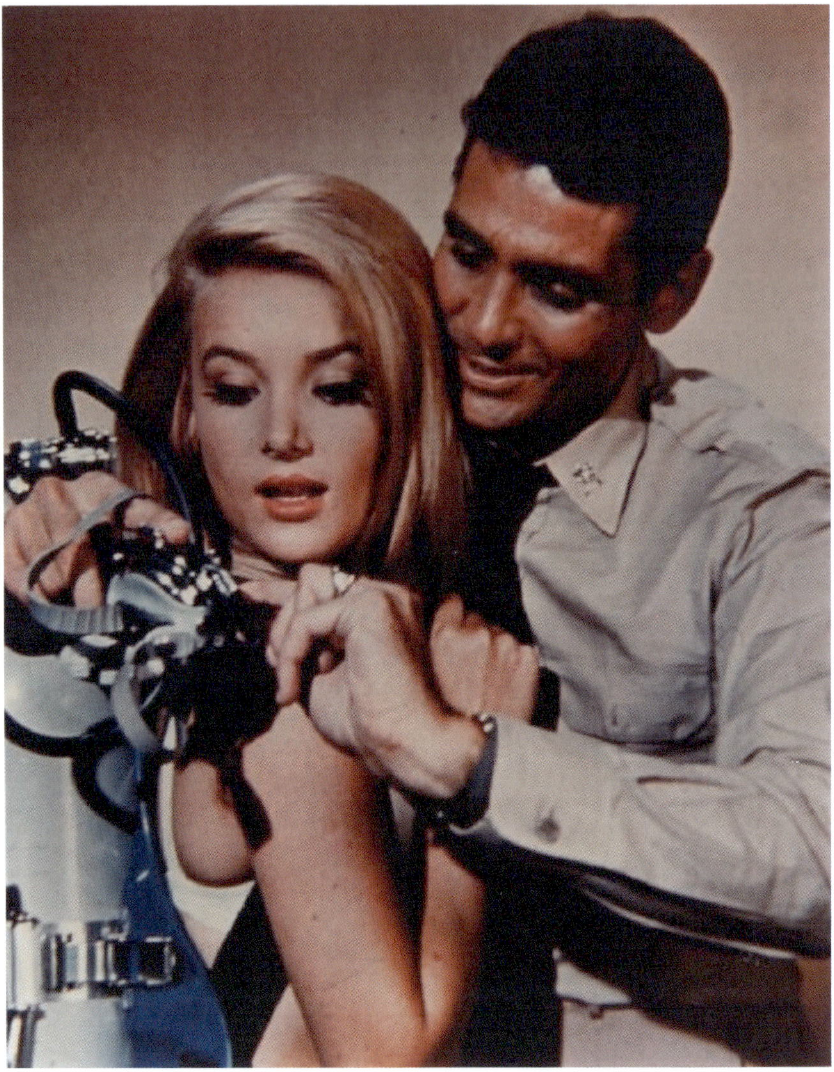

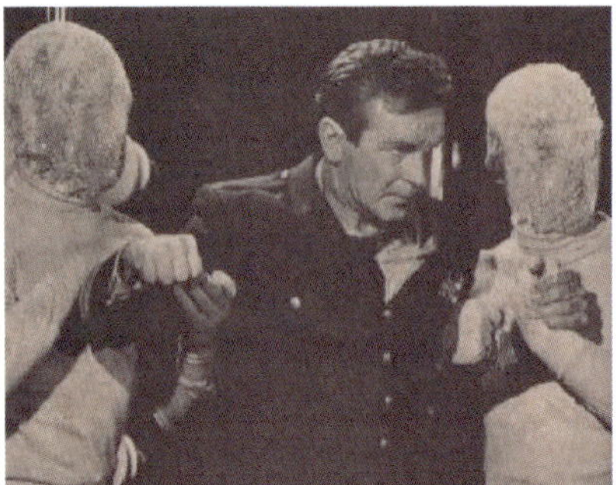

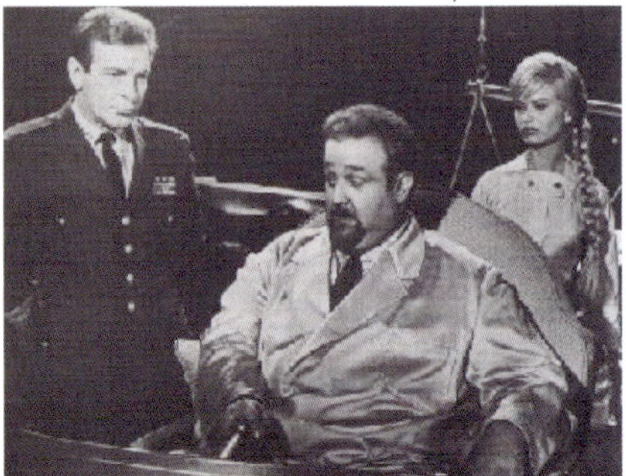

95

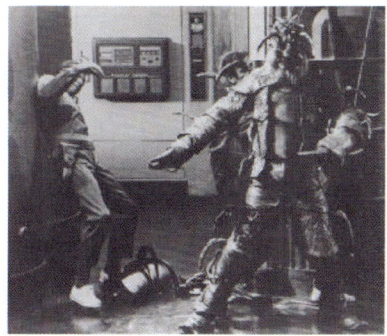

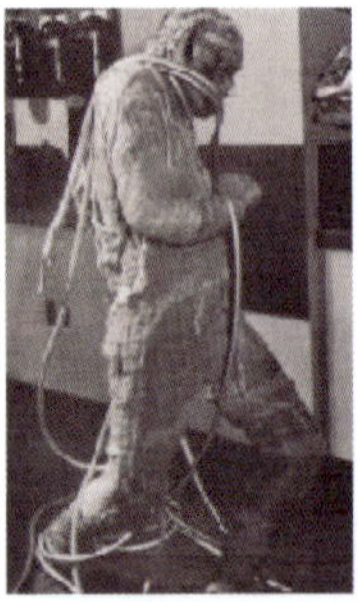
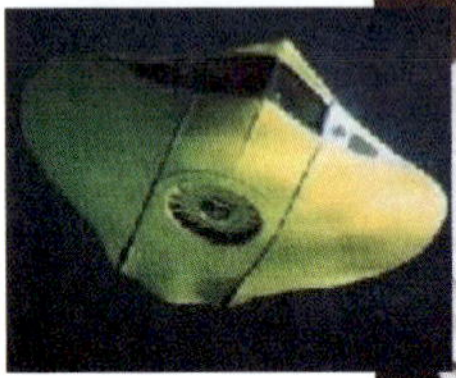
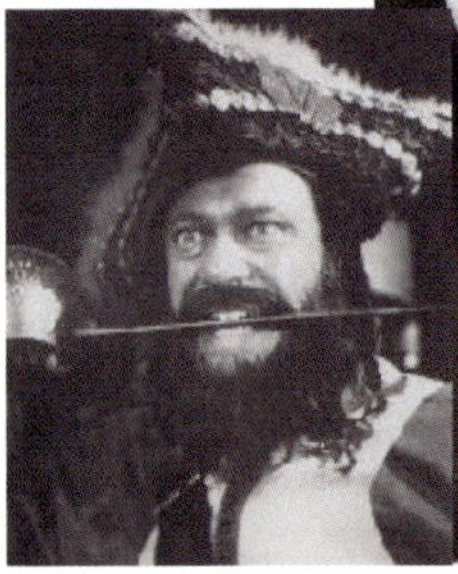
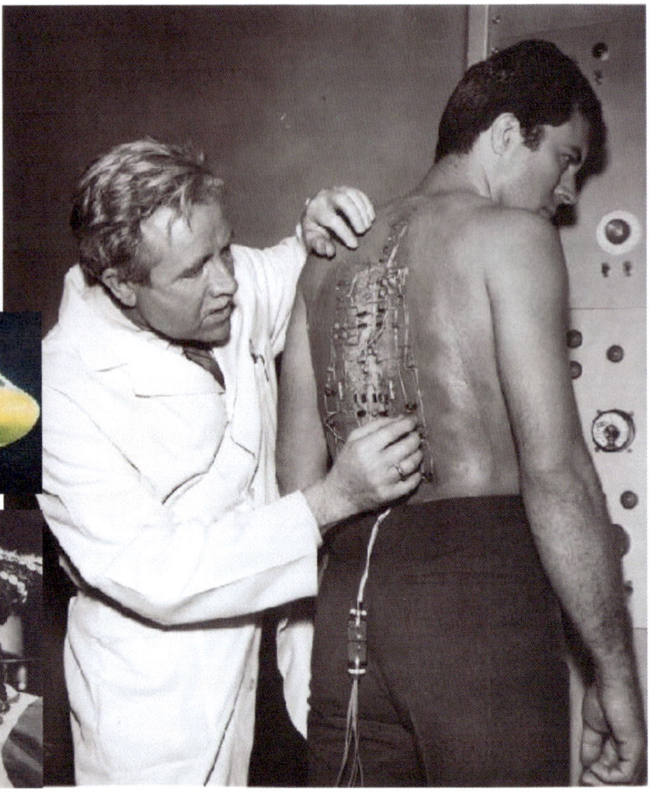
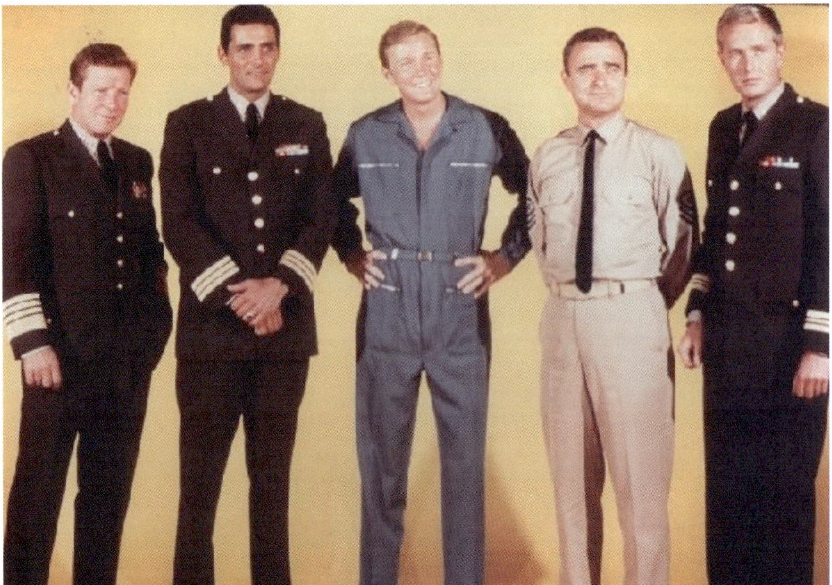

Trick question: Which one of these Lost in Space monsters actually did appear first on Voyage to the Bottom of the Sea? And which two never did?

"Me!"

Above: *David Hedison clowns around with the Lost in Space Cyclops. Below, a light moment on the set filming the ol' rock 'n roll…*

This page and next: beautiful George Wilson artwork for the Voyage to the Bottom of the Sea *comic book series.*

Page 95: "The Lobster Man".

Page 96: James Darren as an android in the clumsily titled "The Mechanical Man". Plus, "The Mummy" and "Return of Blackbeard".

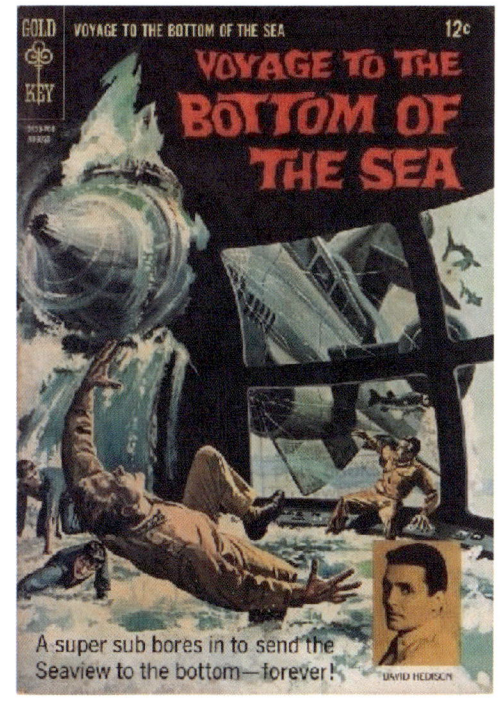

Top left, the first season's "The Sky is Falling", above. David Hedison fools around with Barbara Bouchet (the end result of the photo shoot can be found on page 94; at no point was a bikini and diving gear essential to the plot! Nice one, Lee…).

99

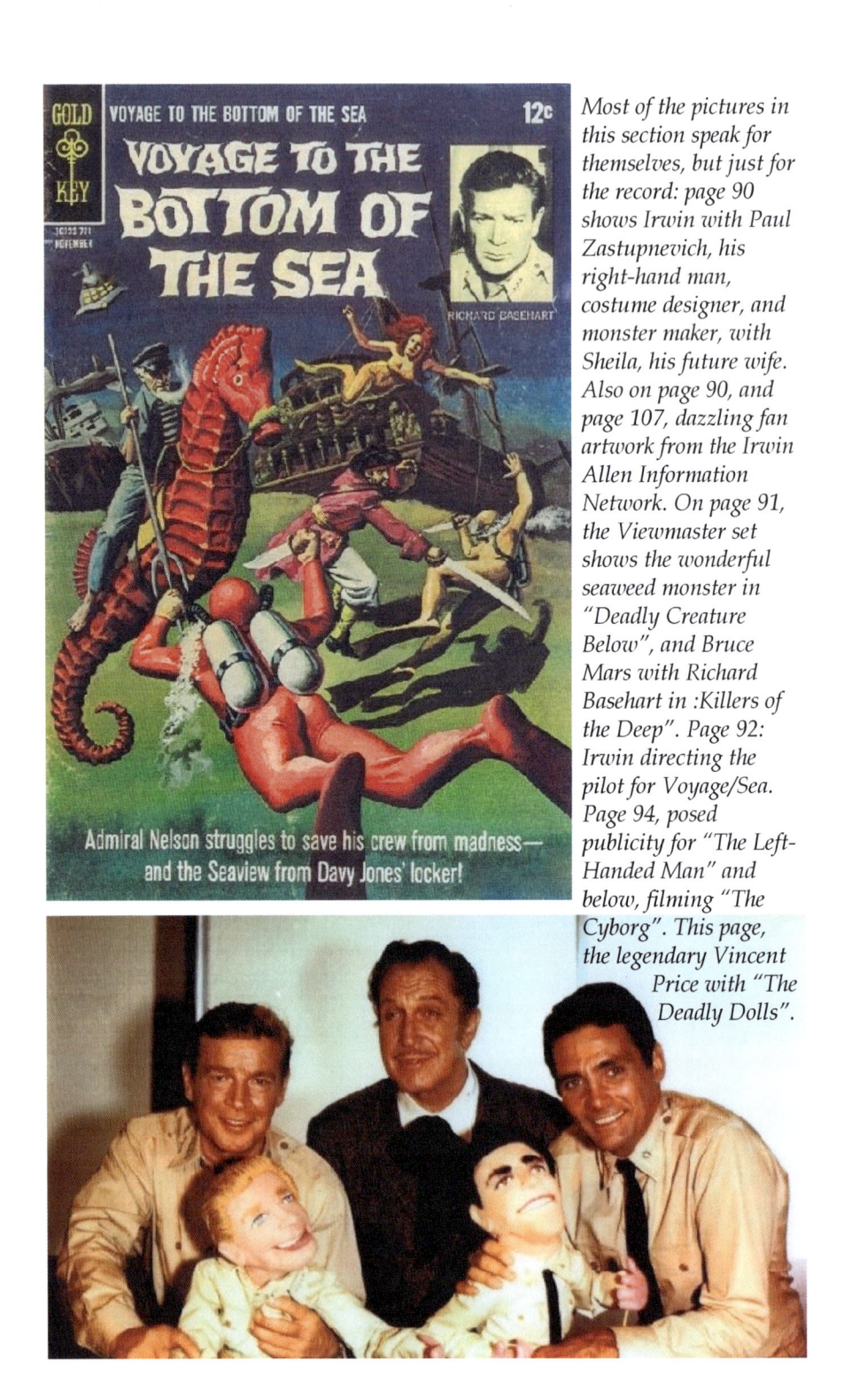

Most of the pictures in this section speak for themselves, but just for the record: page 90 shows Irwin with Paul Zastupnevich, his right-hand man, costume designer, and monster maker, with Sheila, his future wife. Also on page 90, and page 107, dazzling fan artwork from the Irwin Allen Information Network. On page 91, the Viewmaster set shows the wonderful seaweed monster in "Deadly Creature Below", and Bruce Mars with Richard Basehart in :Killers of the Deep". Page 92: Irwin directing the pilot for Voyage/Sea. Page 94, posed publicity for "The Left-Handed Man" and below, filming "The Cyborg". This page, the legendary Vincent Price with "The Deadly Dolls".

100

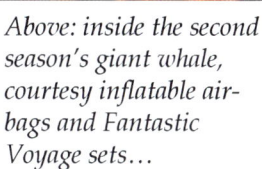

Above: inside the second season's giant whale, courtesy inflatable air-bags and Fantastic Voyage sets…

Following Voyage to the Bottom of the Sea, Irwin went on to make three further classic sci-fi series of the 1960s – the popular and fondly remembered Lost in Space, cult classic The Time Tunnel, and the unearthly Land of the Giants, featured on the following pages…

Aaarrr! Albert Salmi in full pirate mode for "Dead Men's Doubloons"

LOST
IN
SPACE

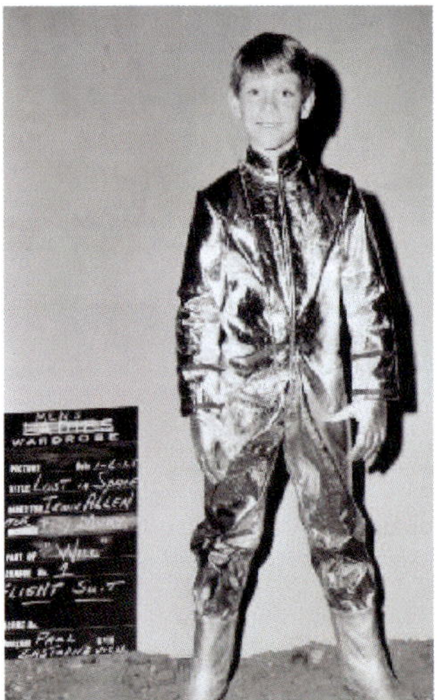

LOST IN SPACE
ROBOT
MOTORIZED

IRWIN ALLEN

LOST
IN
SPACE

Clockwise from top left, Mark Goddard, Marta Kristen, June Lockhart, Guy Williams, Angela Cartwright, Billy Mumy.

Previous page: early cast shots and merchandise. This page: Irwin directs the pilot. Page 108: Angela Cartwright meets Adam West.

105

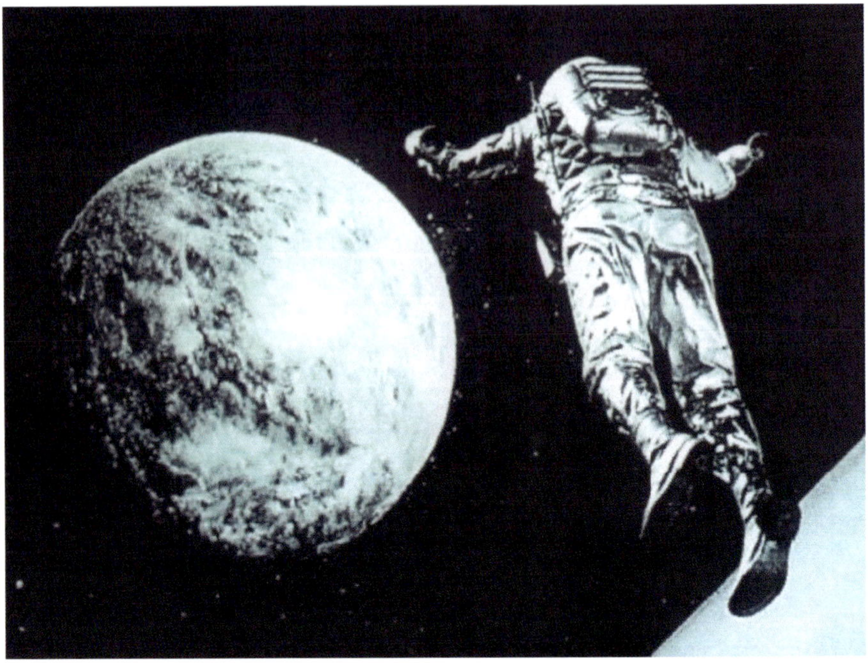

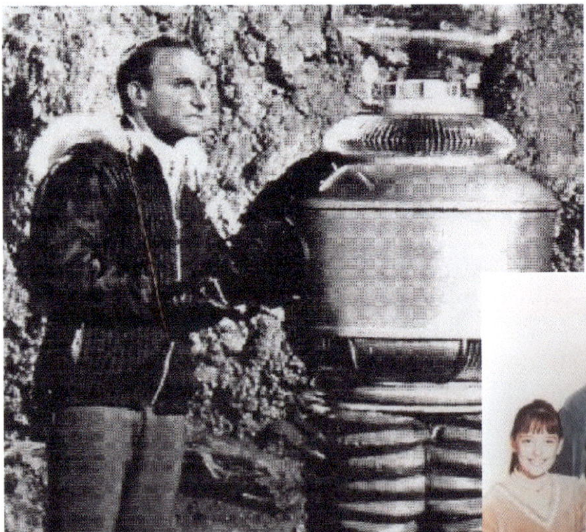

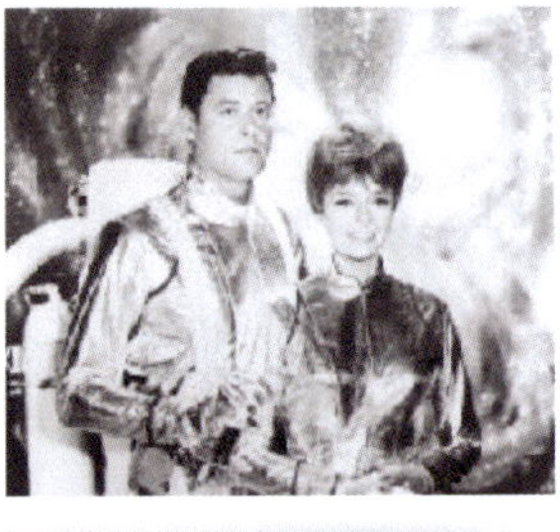

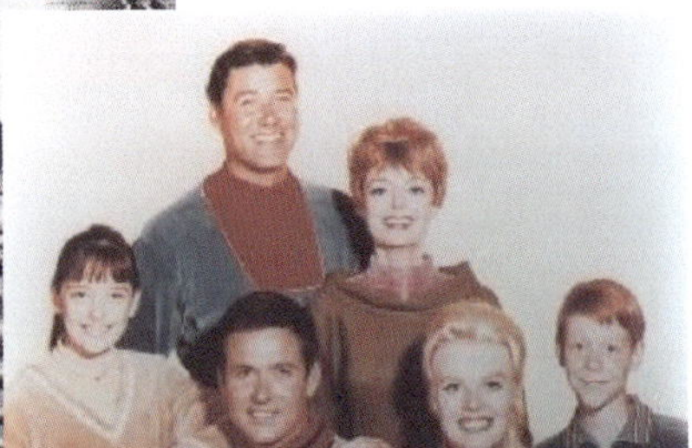

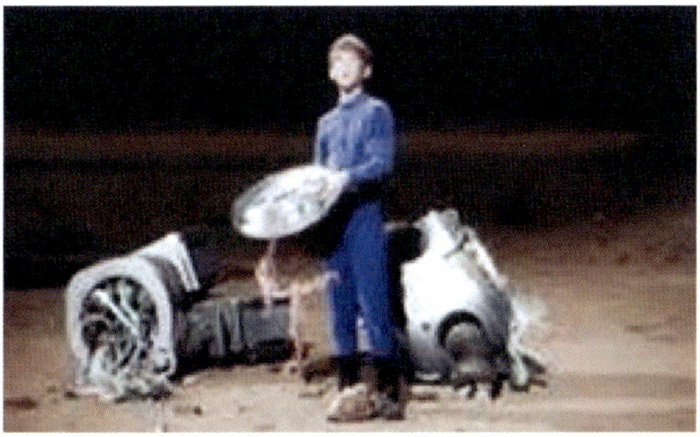

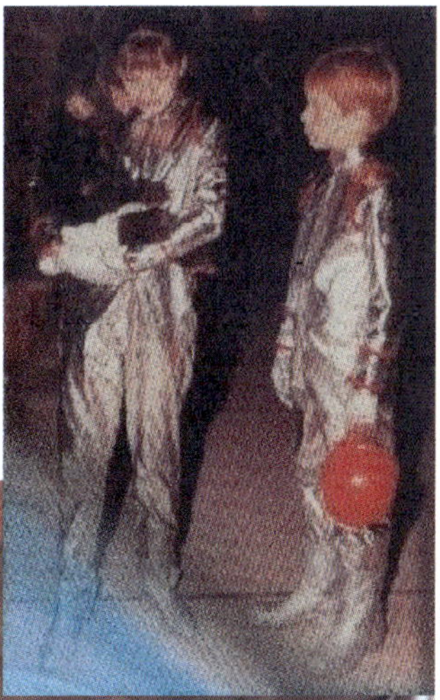

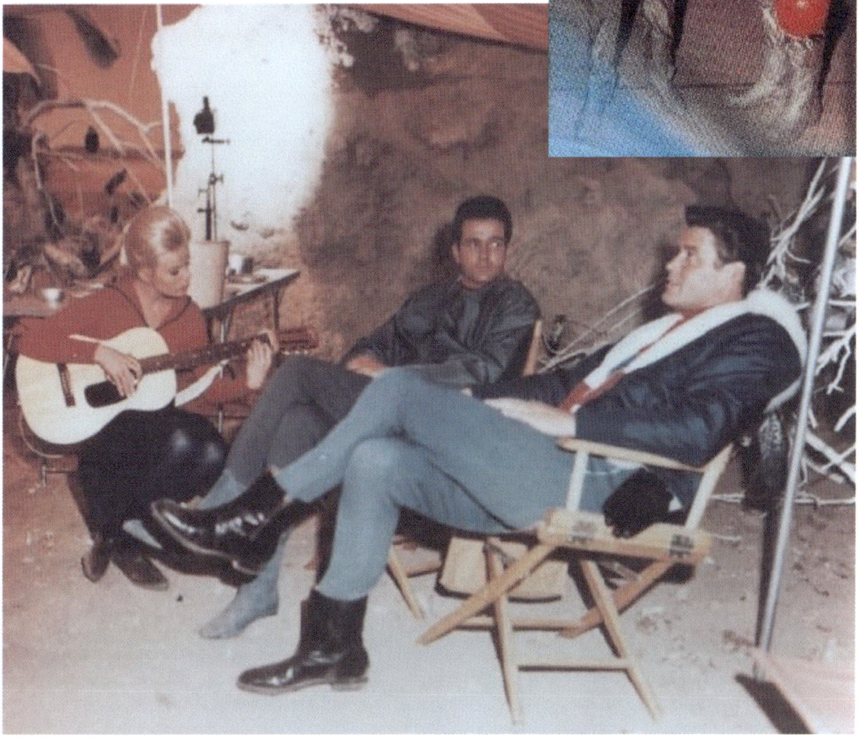

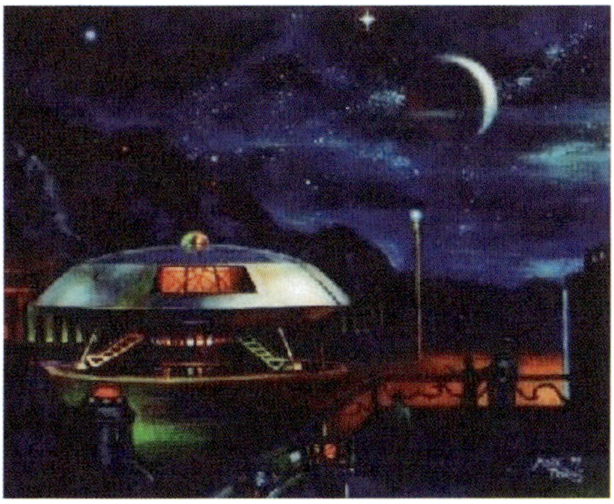

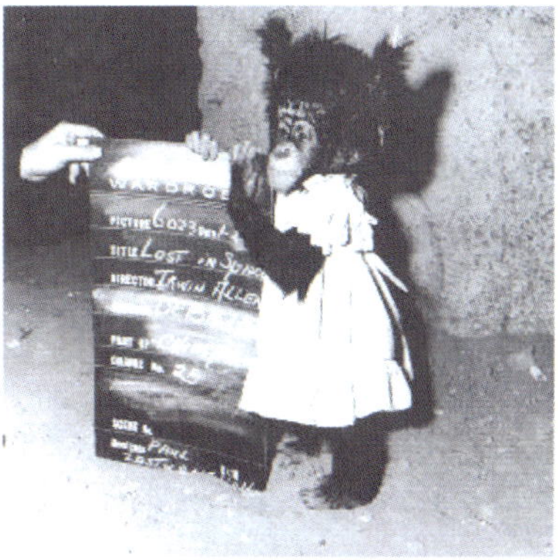

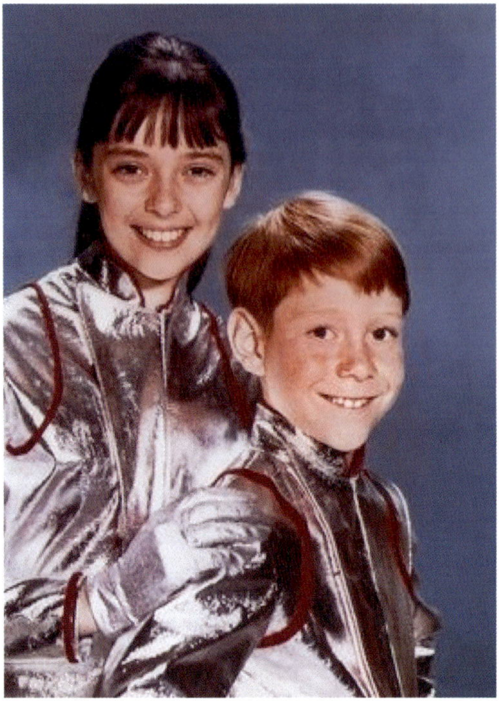
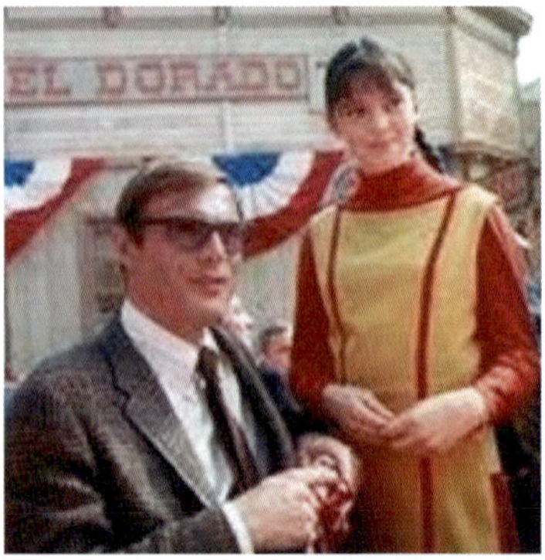
EL DORADO
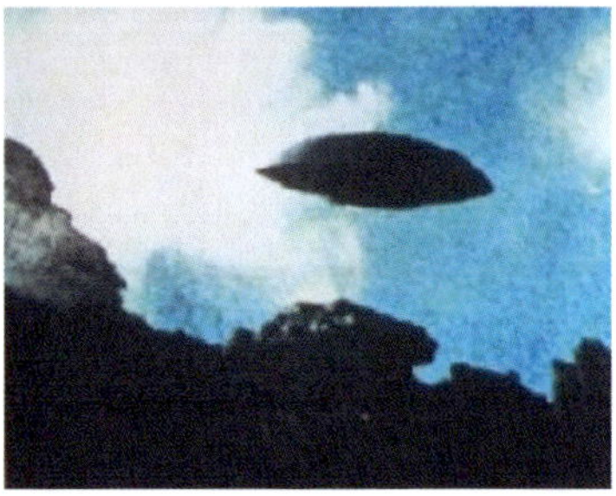
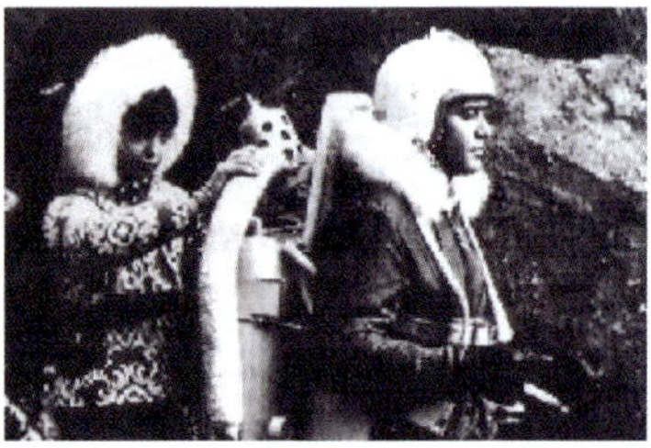
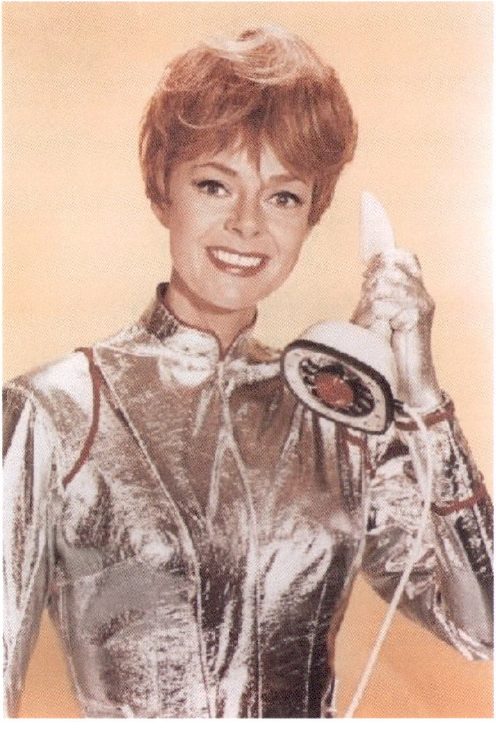
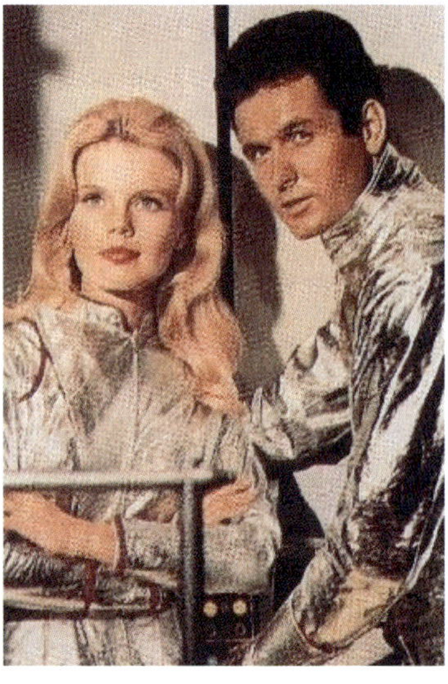

Enter Jonathan Harris as Doctor Smith… Initially a smarmy villain brought in to goose the show, he and the Robot (Bobby May) became comedic characters, as shown on pages 112 – 114.

109

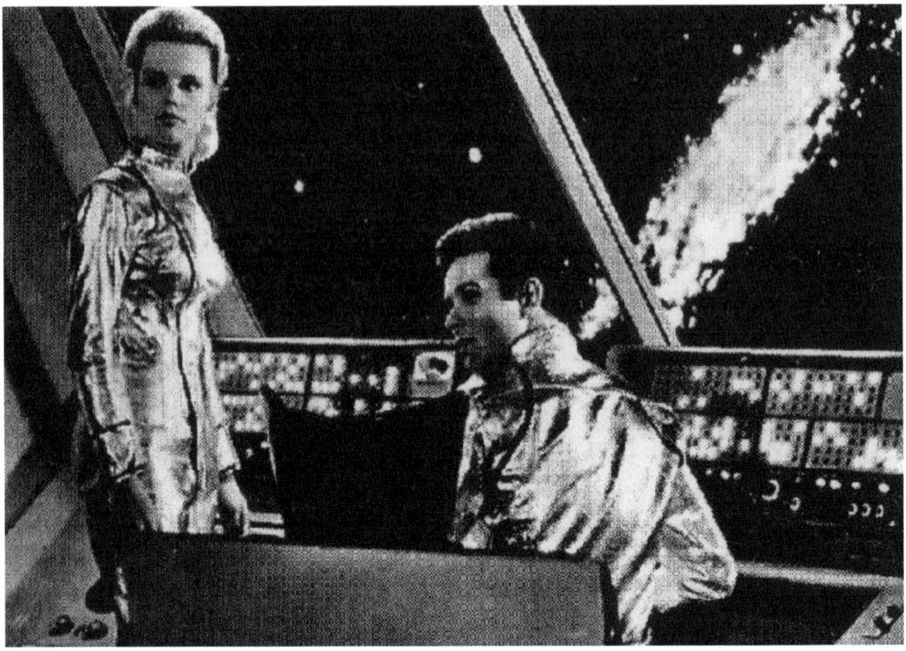

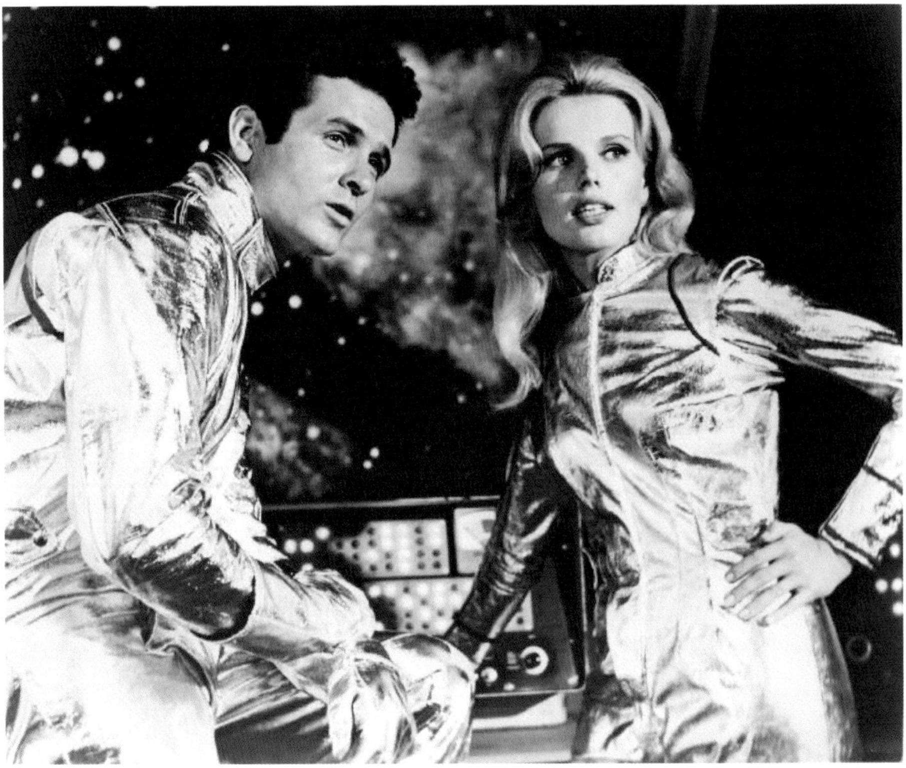

"Invaders From the Fifth Dimension"

112

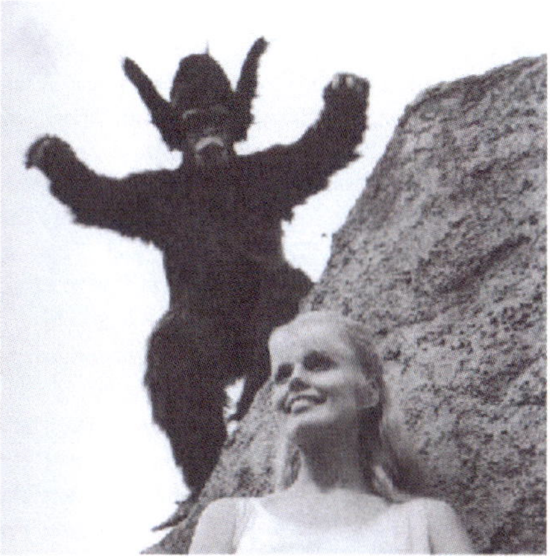

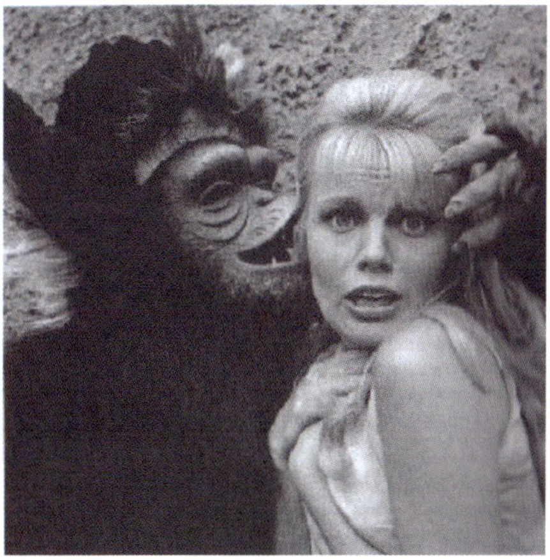

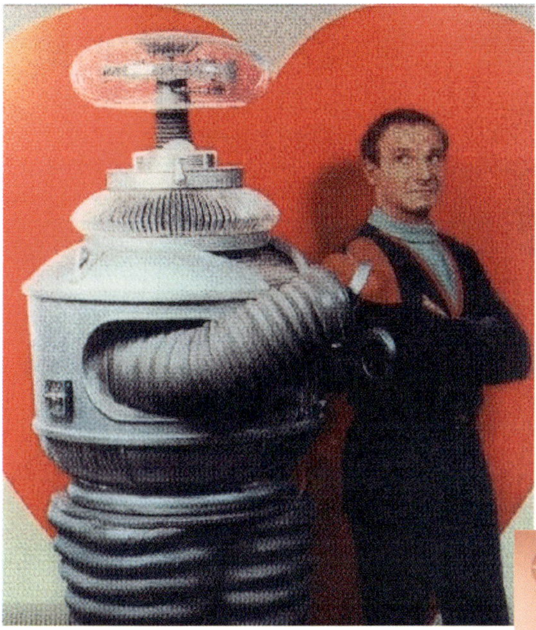

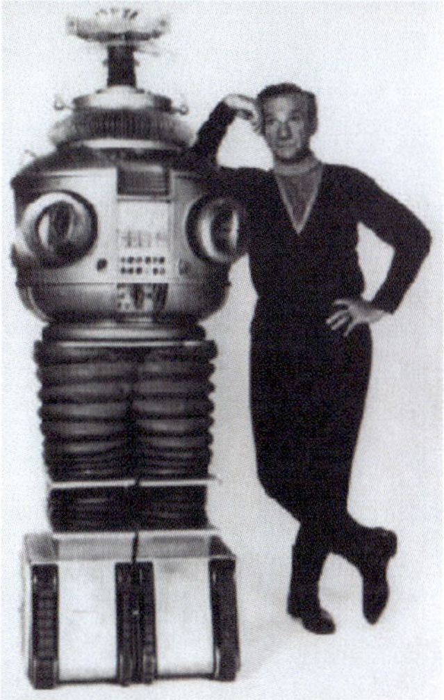

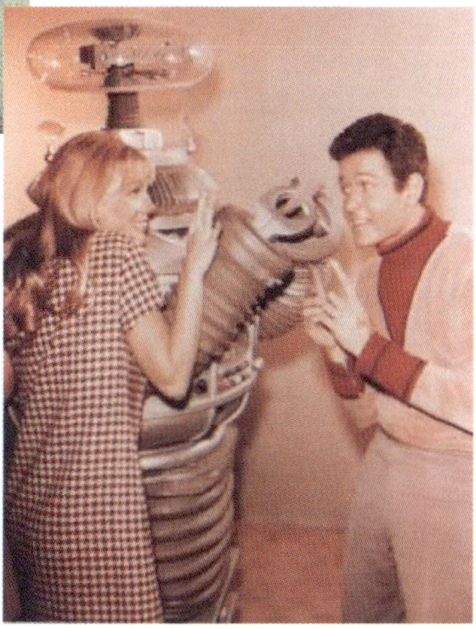

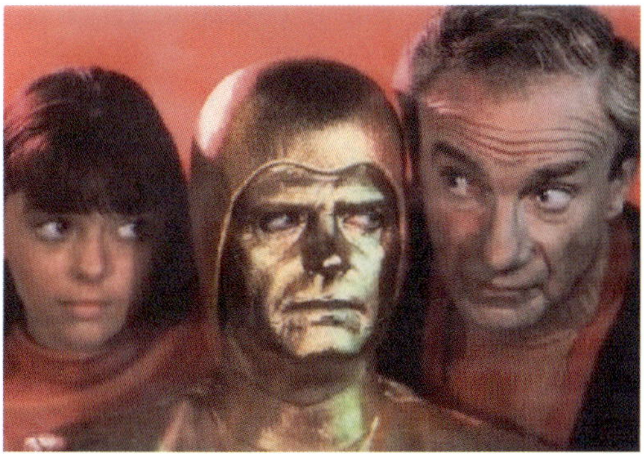

Wonderful publicity shots for the equally wonderful "The Golden Man". Inset: "West of Mars".

114

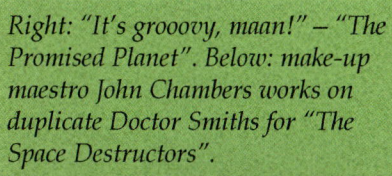

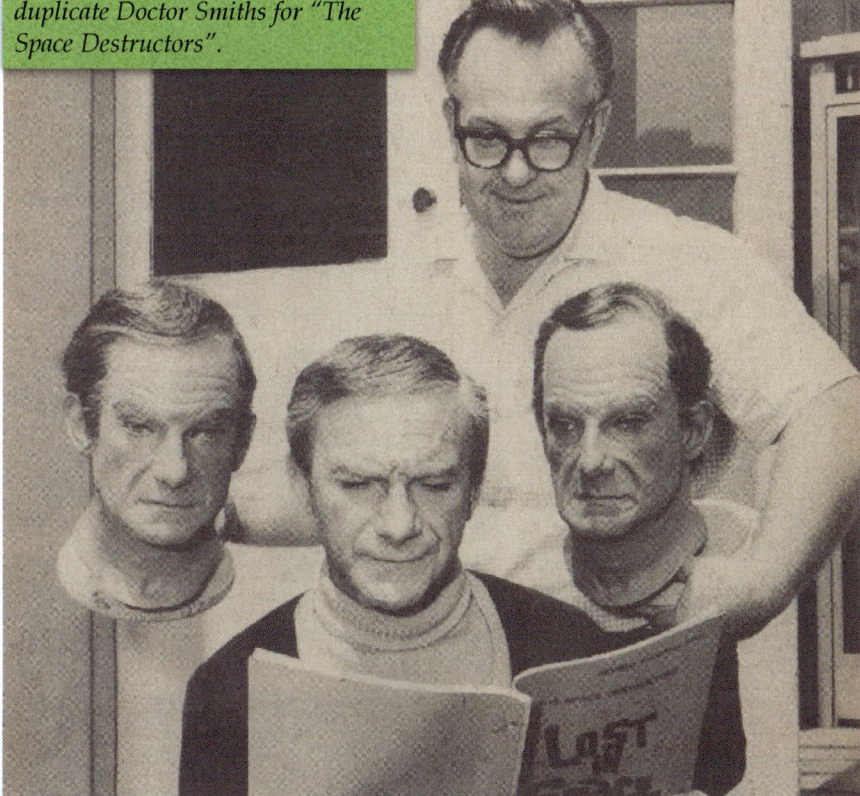

Right: "It's grooovy, maan!" – "The Promised Planet". Below: make-up maestro John Chambers works on duplicate Doctor Smiths for "The Space Destructors".

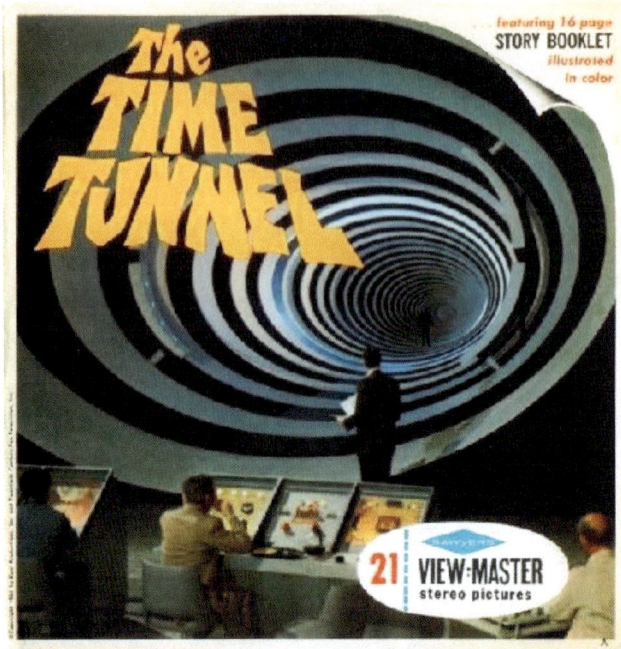

Below: Filming the pilot for The Time Tunnel. Actors Gary Merrill, Whit Bissell, and Robert Colbert are standing bottom left.

Next page: Lee Meriwether and Robert Colbert pose on the set. Note the floor with logo isn't in yet.

Bottom left, one of the series' elaborate miniature composites.

117

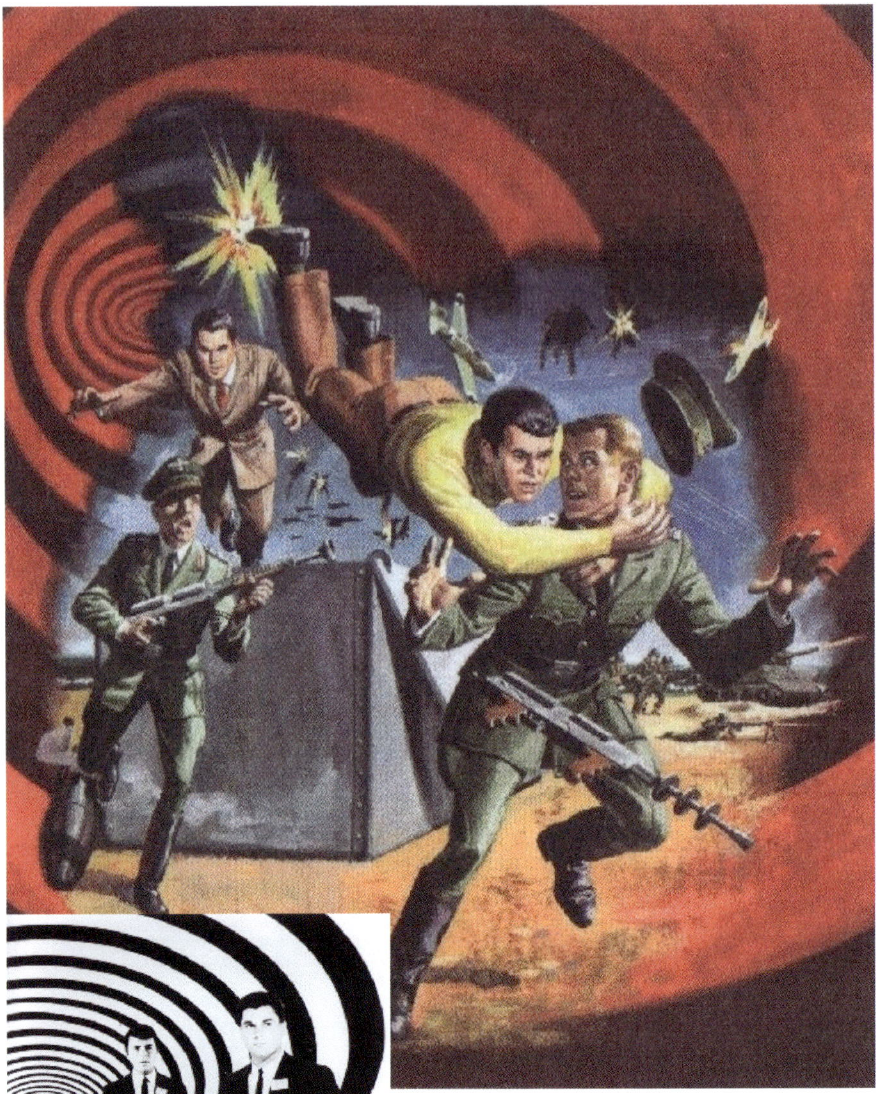

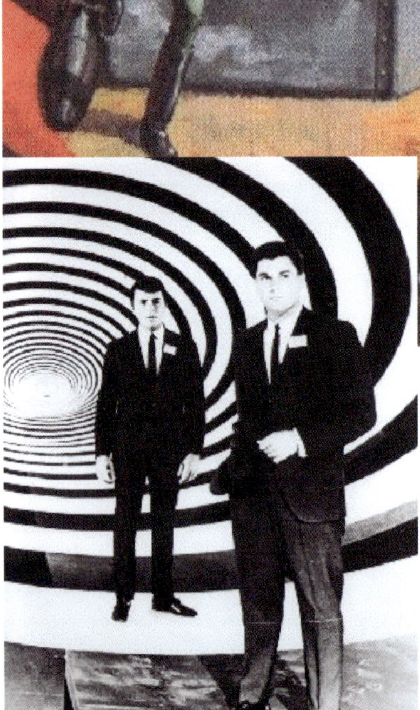

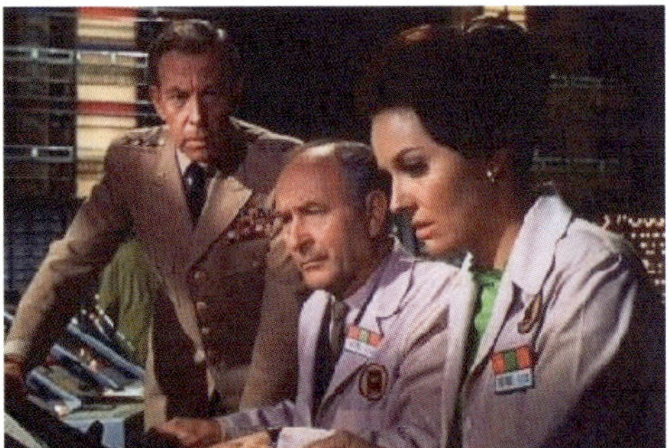

Scenes from the pilot for Land of the Giants, "The Crash". Gary Conway and Deanna Lund are menaced by Don Watters.

120

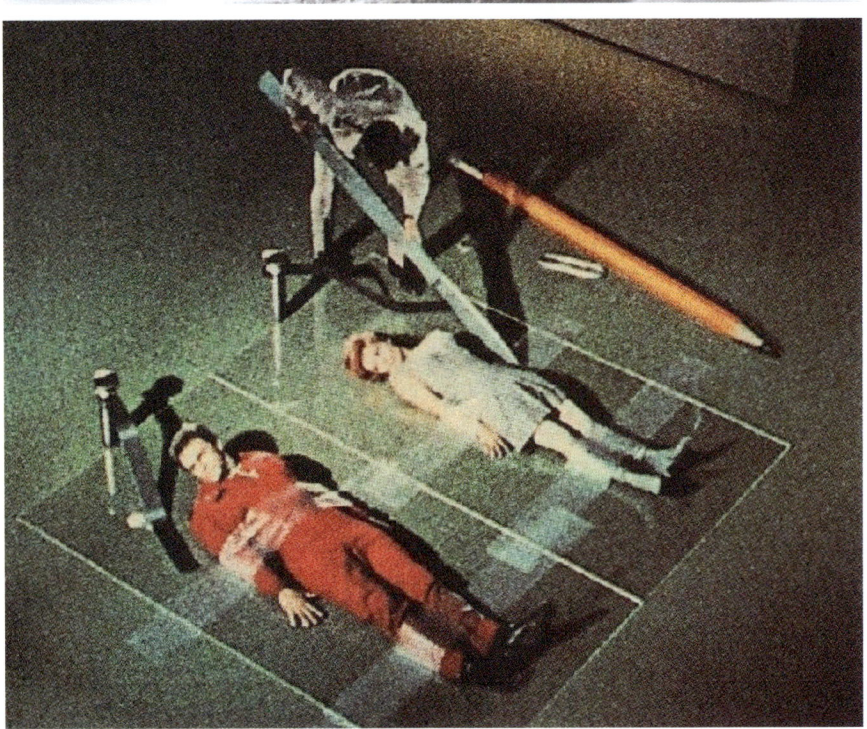

121

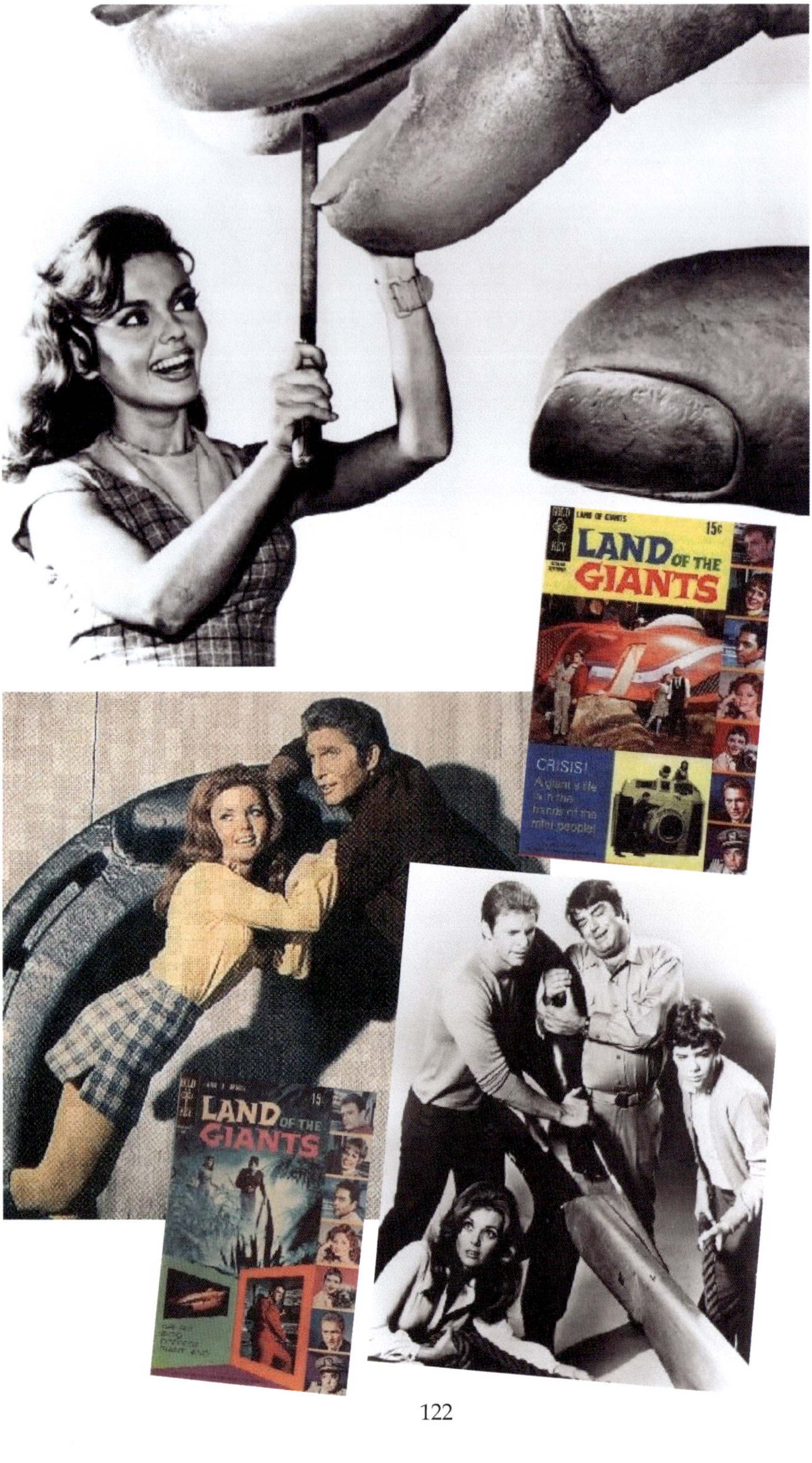
15¢
LAND OF THE GIANTS
CRISIS!
LAND OF THE GIANTS
15¢

123

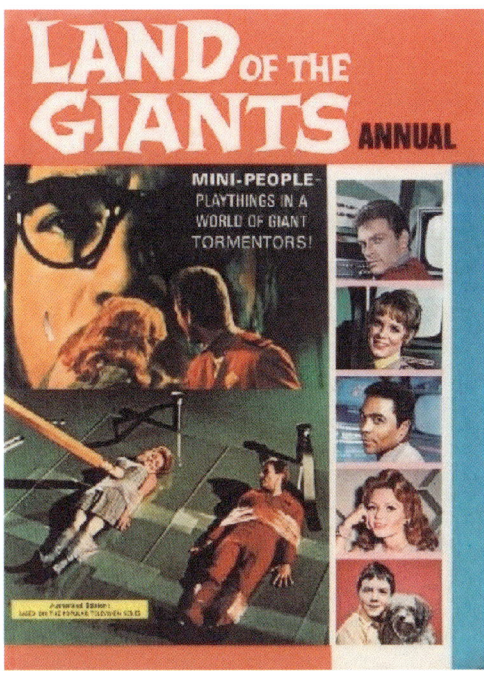

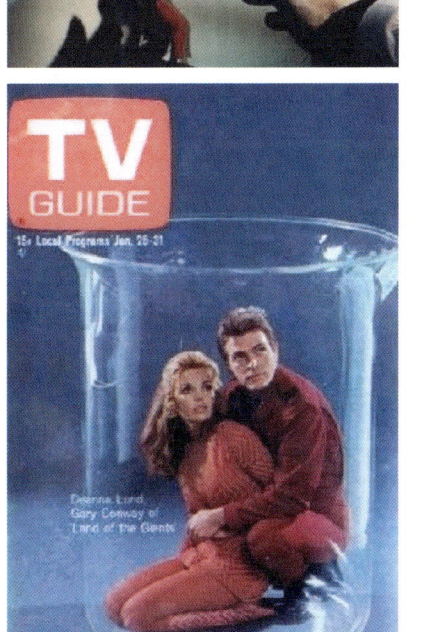

"Okay… look up… you're concerned… and cut!"; lighter moments on the set of Land of the Giants, with Deanna Lund and Kurt Kasznar above, and Stefan Arngrim, Gary Conway, Don Marshall, and Heather Young below.

125

"Only in the '60s" Movies

Jane Fonda and David Hemmings in Barbarella.

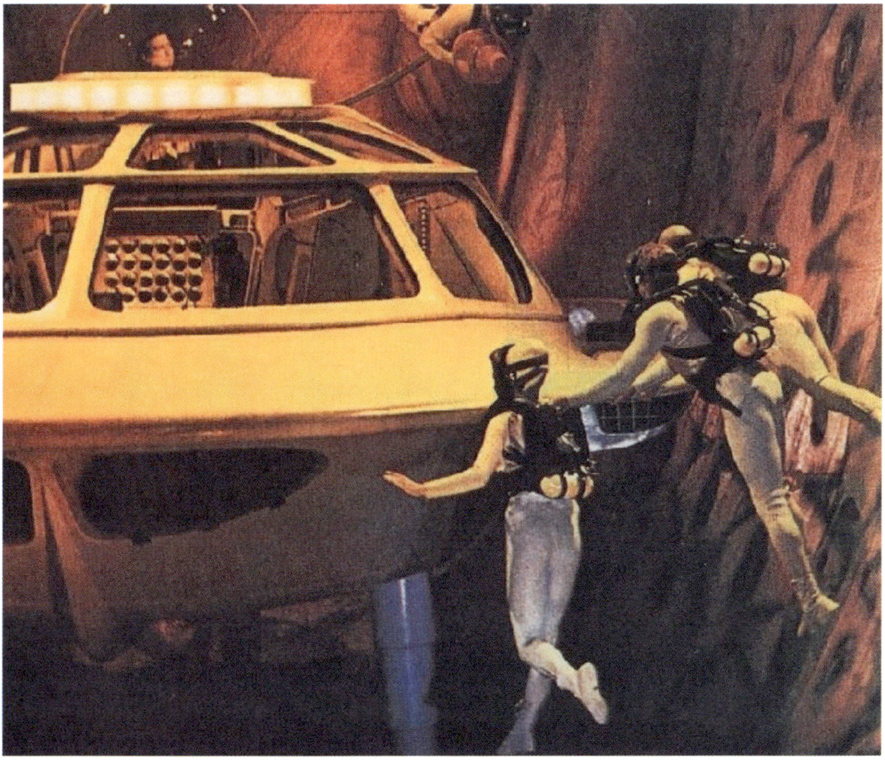

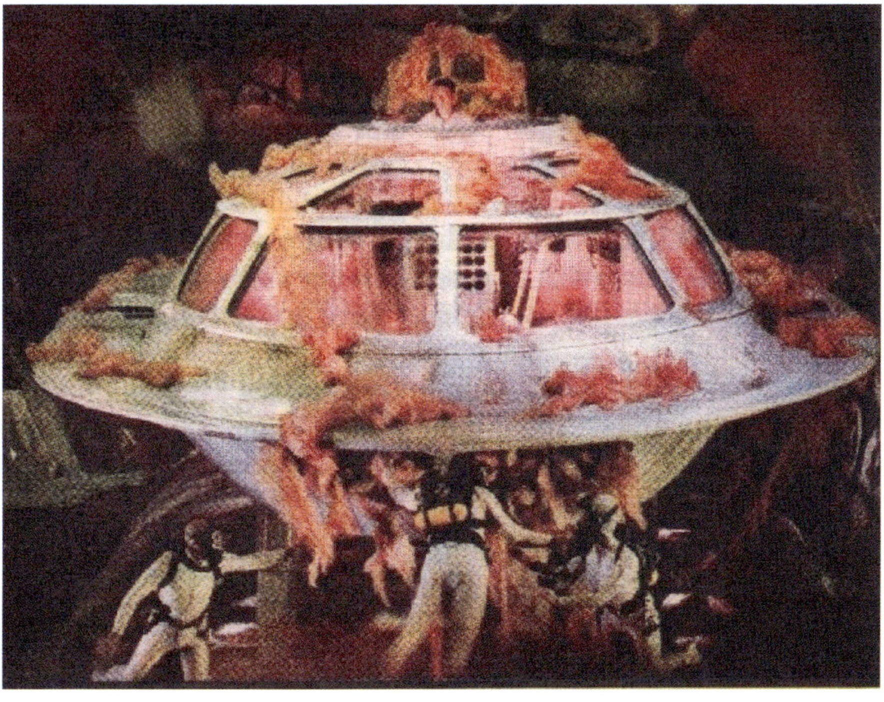

This page and previous, Fantastic Voyage.

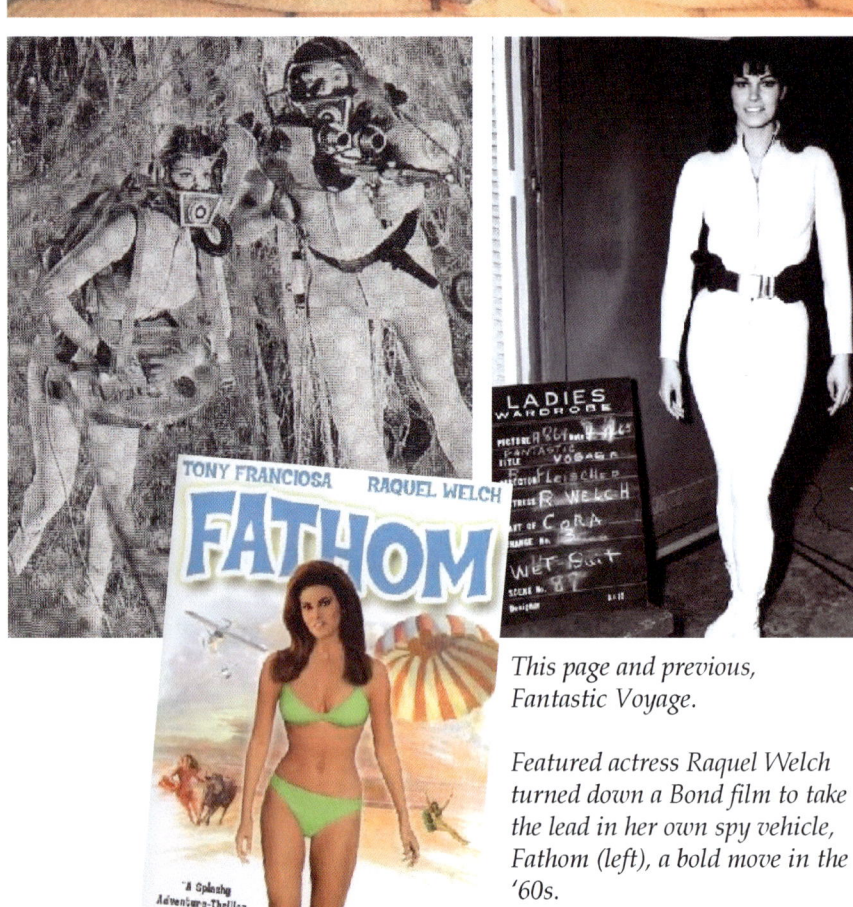

Featured actress Raquel Welch turned down a Bond film to take the lead in her own spy vehicle, Fathom (left), a bold move in the '60s.

128

Top: Joan O'Brien takes charge in Get Yourself a College Girl. Bottom left, Gorgo. Bottom right: Santa Claus Conquers the Martians. I did say only in the '60s…

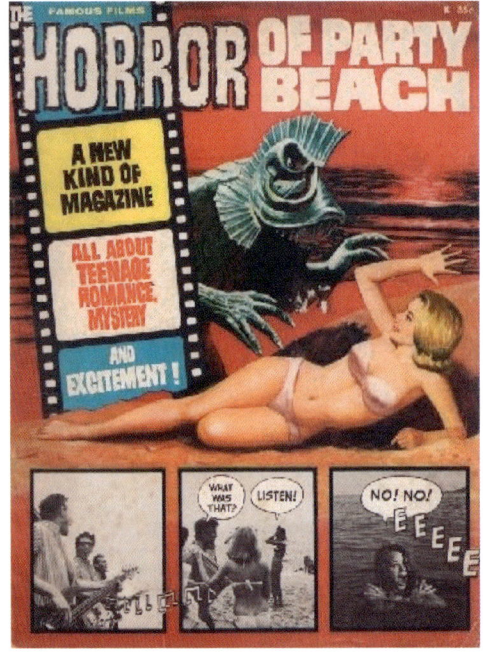

Above: Santa Claus Conquers the Martians.

Above: Surf Party. This page and next: Pajama Party.

Above: Tommy Kirk, Annette Funicello, and Elsa Lanchester in Pajama Party.

Next page: Shelley Fabares and Fabian in Ride the Wild Surf.

If this title turns out to be popular, I'll be back with a follow-up, Spirit of the '60s, Volume 2...

In the meantime, check out my other more text-heavy titles on the following pages, and click on my author's page on Amazon for even more...

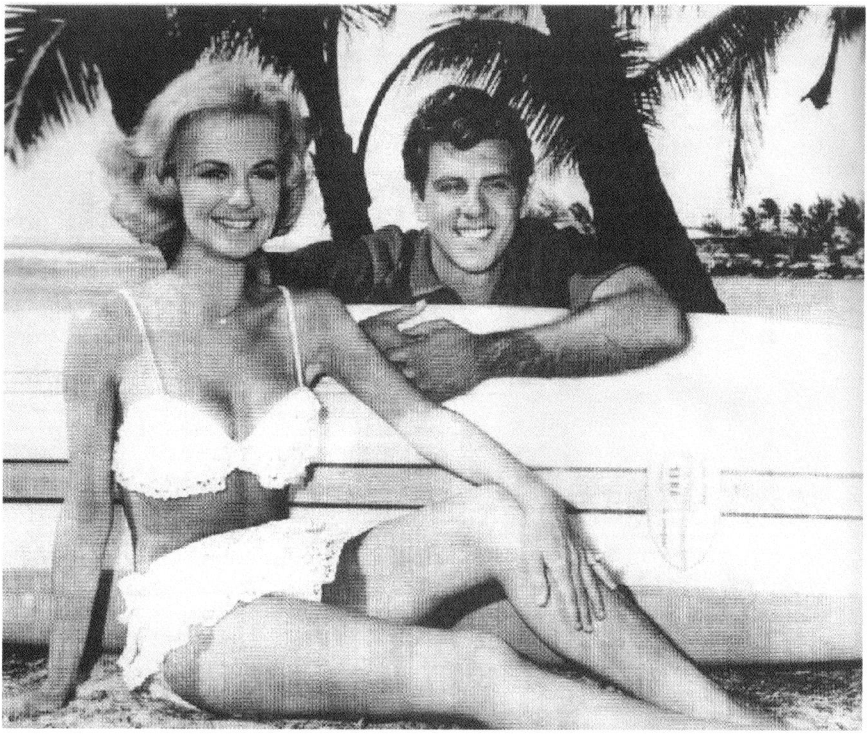

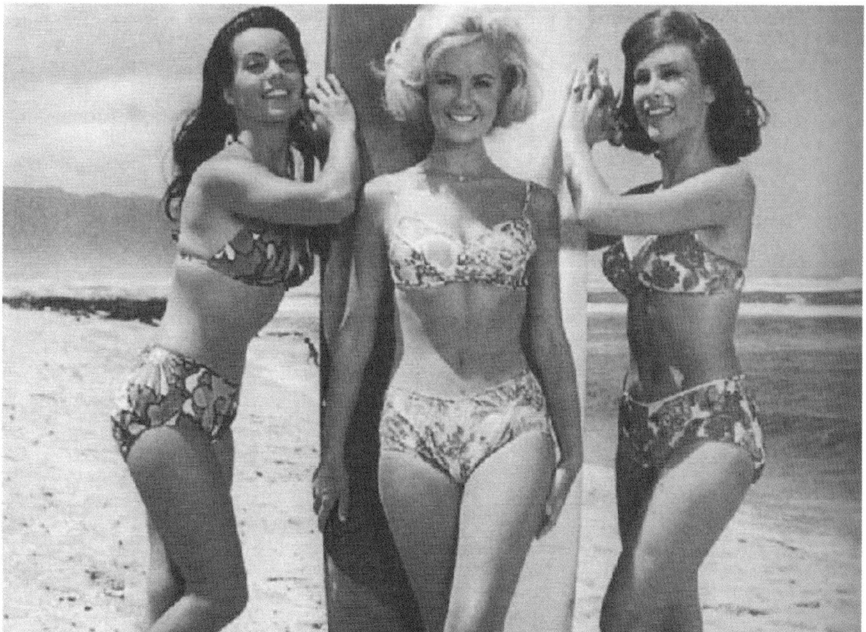

about the author

Jon Abbott was born in Lambeth, London, England, and has lived in Brighton on the South Coast since he was five years old. He has been writing professionally for over thirty years, having started out in 1982 by writing brief previews and reviews for the London listings magazine *City Limits*. For two years he contributed an annual report on the U.S. TV season to the trade paper *Television Weekly* before it was amalgamated with *Broadcast*. Since then, he has written over 400 articles and features for around two dozen different trade, specialist, and populist publications, including numerous regular columns and features.

In 1983, he wrote his first article for the British science-fiction and fantasy media magazine *Starburst*, on the cult series *The Prisoner*. This was followed by features on *The Outer Limits, Danger Man, Voyage to the Bottom of the Sea, The Man from UNCLE, V, The Greatest American Hero, Blue Thunder, Knight Rider, Airwolf, Streethawk, Otherworld, ALF, Batman, Battlestar Galactica, The Time Tunnel, Fantastic Journey, Land of the Giants*, and *The Invisible Man*. For the companion title *TV Zone*, he has written about *Misfits of Science, Beauty and the Beast, Planet of the Apes, Fantastic Journey, Quantum Leap*, supernatural anthology shows, *Starman, Man from Atlantis, The Incredible Hulk, Spider-Man, Logan's Run, The Invaders, The Avengers*, and *Hercules--the Legendary Journeys*.

For six years he wrote TV news and individual features for *Video Today* in the popular column *Time-Shift*, which he proposed in 1984 and which became one of the most well-received features in the magazine. These pages included previews of new shows, retrospectives on popular old series, genre pieces, and regular updates on the U.S. TV scene. He wrote individual features on *Night Gallery, Dallas, Dynasty, Soap, The Mary Tyler Moore Show, Hill Street Blues, Mike Hammer*, Britain's Euston Films, producers Donald Bellisario and Quinn Martin, *Bilko, V, The Invaders, Cheers, Police Squad, Lou Grant, The A-Team, Crazy Like a Fox, The Equalizer, The Prisoner, The Twilight Zone, Lost in Space, L.A. Law, Moonlighting, Mission: Impossible, Star Trek--the Next Generation, The Time Tunnel*, supernatural anthology shows, the anti-violence-on-TV lobby, and the arrival of satellite TV. He also reviewed video releases. Particularly successful were the occasional TV Index features listing the status of then-current American shows both in the U.S. and the U.K.

Between October 1984 and March 1986 he wrote a regular column of criticism and comment on U.K. scheduling policy for the highly regarded industry journal *Stills*, and from September 1986 he had a number of features on program planning developments in British, American and satellite TV published in *Media Week*. These features covered such issues as the program scheduling strategies of ITV, the birth and growth of Sky Television, a comparison of the original SuperChannel and Sky satellite services, the U.S. TV seasons, video releases of popular television series, merchandising spin-offs from television series, how British broadcasters used imported American programmes in their schedules, the perils of sponsorship and the American experience, television censorship, the merger of satellite broadcasters Sky and BSB, and the purchase of MTM by U.K. broadcaster TVS.

In 1988 he began contributing to *What Satellite* magazine, writing features on such shows as *The Legend of Custer, Hawk, Lost in Space, 21, Jump Street, St. Elsewhere, Murphy Brown, The Flash, Melrose Place, Beverly Hills 90210*, Steven Bochco's *Civil Wars*, Stephen Cannell's *Stingray, The Simpsons, Land of the Giants, Tom and Jerry, Taxi, Cheers, Frasier* and *The Twilight Zone*.

For *The Dark Side*, a horror and sci-fi magazine, he has provided features on *Alien Nation, The Outer Limits, Werewolf, Land of the Giants, Star Trek, Star Trek--the Next Generation, Voyage to the Bottom of the Sea, Lost in Space,* the Stephen King mini-series *It, The Flash,* and *The X-Files.*

For *Video Buyer* he covered the video release of *Star Trek, V, The Avengers, Robin of Sherwood, Doctor Who,* the Marvel Video Comics, '50s sci-fi films, the early *Superman* serials and TV shows, the output of the Hanna-Barbera and Warner Brothers animation studios, *The Outer Limits, The Twilight Zone,* and *Twin Peaks*. For *Video World* he covered the video release of *Lost in Space, Cheers, The Simpsons,* and *Twin Peaks* and wrote their *Satellite Preview* column, which has included features on *Beverly Hills 90210, The New Avengers, Charlie's Angels, MASH, Twin Peaks,* Robin Hood films, *Quantum Leap, Lou Grant, Star Trek--Voyager, Earth 2, The Invaders, Kolchak--the Night Stalker, Planet of the Apes, Alien Nation, Automan, Manimal, Starsky and Hutch, Murder One, The X-Files,* modern westerns, *Space--Above and Beyond, Bewitched, Star Trek: Deep Space Nine, Starman, Strange Luck,* and *Hercules--the Legendary Journeys.*

In November 1989 he was awarded a special commendation for his writing on American TV and satellite TV in *Media Week* from the first *Broadcast Journalist Awards*, sponsored by TV-am.

During 1990 and 1991 he produced the column *Broadcast News*, a monthly collection of strange stories, anecdotes, and comment and criticism on television for *What Video* magazine.

In 1995, he was asked to contribute a monthly TV news column for *Home Entertainment,* and also wrote additional features on the U.S. TV season, the Cartoon Network and TNT, and Bravo's '*Weird Worlds*' strip. He was also invited to join the writing team of *SFX*, for which he reviewed *Robocop--the series, The X-Files, Sliders, Highlander,* and *Space: Above and Beyond*. For '*Yesterday's Heroes*', a regular monthly feature in the early issues of *SFX*, he featured *The Six Million Dollar Man, Wonder Woman, Blue Thunder,*

The Invisible Man, Randall and Hopkirk (Deceased), UFO, The Time Tunnel, Manimal, Max Headroom, The Man from UNCLE, Voyage to the Bottom of the Sea, Starman, V, Batman, Mission: Impossible, The Incredible Hulk and *Land of the Giants*. For another then-new publication, *Cult Times*, he wrote about *Earth 2, The Six Million Dollar Man, Kolchak--the Night Stalker*, and *Sliders*.

In 1996, he was invited to write for the SF media magazine *Dreamwatch* and the new publications *Infinity* and *Comedy Review*. For *Comedy Review*, he prepared features and episode listings for the series *Soap* and *MASH*. For *Infinity*, he wrote a monthly *Cult TV* column and contributed articles on *The X-Files, War of the Worlds--the series, Space--Above and Beyond, V, Star Trek: Deep Space Nine, Dark Skies* and *Lois and Clark: New Adventures of Superman*. For *Dreamwatch*, he wrote about *The Green Hornet*, the *Fantasy Worlds of Irwin Allen* documentary, *The X-Files*, sci-fi in *The Simpsons, Fantastic Journey, The Man from Atlantis, Fireball XL-5*, the 1950s *Superman* series, and *The Pretender*. His exclusive reviews of *Millennium* and *Dark Skies* were the first published in the U.K.

Over a five year period between 1997 and 2001, he covered over forty episodes of different vintage sci-fi series for the '*Fantasy Flashback*' series for *TV Zone*, which featured an individual episode of a classic TV fantasy series examined in detail. Shows covered included *Star Trek, The Outer Limits, The Time Tunnel, Lost in Space, Batman, Voyage to the Bottom of the Sea, Mork and Mindy, Battlestar Galactica, The Greatest American Hero, Once a Hero, The Flash, Land of the Giants, Otherworld, The Man from UNCLE, The Wild Wild West, Airwolf, Kolchak--the Night Stalker, The Invaders, Thunderbirds, Quantum Leap, Mission: Impossible, Bewitched, The Flintstones, The Twilight Zone, Streethawk*, and *I Dream of Jeannie*. He also reviewed third season *Stargate* for *TV Zone*, and later wrote a '*Retro TV*' column for *TV Zone* covering all aspects of classic TV.

In 2006, American publishers McFarland published his book *Irwin Allen Television Productions 1964-1970*, a detailed critical review of the 1960s sci-fi series *Lost in Space, Voyage to the Bottom of the Sea, The Time Tunnel*, and *Land of the Giants*, and in 2009 *Stephen J. Cannell Television Productions: A History of All Series and Pilots*, a critical study of 22 detective and action adventure series from this prolific producer, including *The Rockford Files, The A-Team*, and *Wiseguy*. Also in 2009, the Irwin Allen book was reprinted in softback.

Now concentrating solely on 20th century film and TV, and self-publishing on Amazon's Createspace platform, he has published *The Elvis Films* in 2014, *Cool TV of the 1960s: Three Shows That Changed the World*, and *Strange New World: Sex Films of the 1970s* in 2015, *One Hundred of the Best, Most Violent Films Ever* and *The Great Desilu Series of the 1960s* in 2016, and *Cool TV 2: More Cult TV from the 1960s* in 2017.

also available from the same author

The Elvis Films

When a man single-handedly changes the course of popular music with one of the most pure and passionate original sounds of the 20th century, it's tough to care about his sideline occupations. But Elvis Presley wanted to be an actor as much, if not more, as he wanted to be a singer. Many Elvis fans didn't like his movies, and neither did Elvis, very much. And yet, the vast majority of them were box office smashes, sure-fire money making hits. *Someone* was buying tickets. In the 1960s, it seemed *everyone* was buying tickets.

This book considers Elvis Presley's films not as an unwelcome intrusion into the insular Presley universe, even though this is how Presley and his associates usually viewed them, but as a significant part of the late 1950s and primarily 1960s pop culture they represented. Elvis Presley, after all, loved film and TV. *The Elvis Films* puts these guilty pleasures into context with not only Presley's life and circumstances at the time, but looks at how they related—or in some cases did not relate to—the other popular culture of the period.

Jon Abbott has been writing about popular culture for over thirty years in a variety of specialist and trade publications, and his kaleidoscopic knowledge of his subject leaves no stone unturned in this provocative and fact-filled analysis of the Elvis movies and the arts and media environment that surrounded them. He is the author of *Irwin Allen Television Productions 1964-1970, Cool TV of the 1960s,* and *Stephen J. Cannell Productions: A History of All Series and Pilots.*

also available from the same author

Irwin Allen Television Productions, 1964—1970

Before establishing himself as the "master of disaster" with the smash hit 1970s films *The Poseidon Adventure* and *The Towering Inferno*, and before there was even CGI, Irwin Allen created four of the most exciting and enduring television sci-fi series of the 1960s—*Voyage to the Bottom of the Sea*, *Lost in Space*, *The Time Tunnel*, and *Land of the Giants*.

Filmed within yards of each other on the busy sound stages and backlots of 20th Century Fox, Allen's shows were one third Jules Verne and Conan Doyle, one third Saturday morning serials, and one third 1950s bug-eyed monster movies. He also had a "house style" created through using the same actors, writers, directors, sets, props, locations and even aliens and monsters that made them 100 percent Irwin Allen. His tricks and techniques, sometimes adapted from earlier sources, others devised by himself and his award-winning special effects teams, have influenced other productions from *Star Trek* through to the present day.

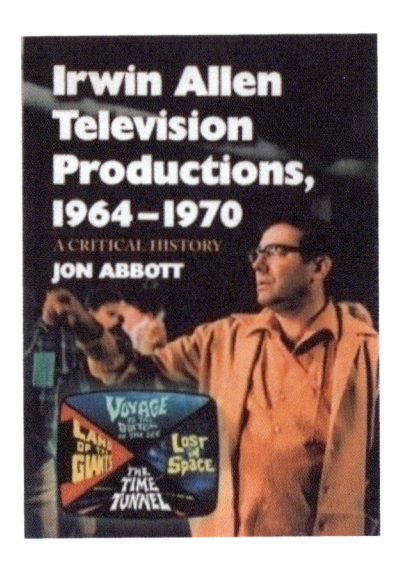

Allen's imprint is everywhere on fantasy TV. Every SF TV show owes him something, and yet none have matched his series for pace, excitement, innovation, or originality. If it was eloquence, scientific accuracy, or profound commentary on the meaning of life you were looking for, then it was best not to look in Irwin Allen productions—but for superb special effects of the day, excellent sets, superior guest performances, action and adventure, hard-nosed heroes, horrible monsters, sinister villains, and sheer escapism, then Irwin was the go-to guy. When Irwin Allen's series were good, they were great. And when they were bad (and sometimes they were)—they were great fun.

This book—a critical history, written by a lifelong fan—documents and examines in detail the premise and origin of each show, and discusses fairly and objectively all 274 episodes of his four fantasy TV series, all of which promoted and perpetuated the traditions and trademarks of pulp sci-fi on film.

also available from the same author

Cool TV of the 1960s: Three shows that Changed the World

It was perhaps synchronicity, everything in the right place at the right time. After Prohibition, the Depression, WWII, and McCarthyism, mainstream America wanted some fun—in color. The post-War world was ready for a New Age and new ideas, for which Elvis and JFK had paved the way. When pop music, the art world, and the fashion world told the rest of the world to lighten up and loosen up, the timing was right. Television followed other aspects of popular culture just as enthusiastically as the public did—and the buzzword of 1960s popular culture and media was NEW! NEW! NEW!

The 1960s was an extraordinary time of creativity for television, with over thirty classic shows on the air in the mid-1960s simultaneously. September 1964 had seen the debut of secret agent show *The Man from UNCLE*, which in 1965, soared up the ratings to become an all-media phenomenon, influencing toys, books, comics, film, fashion, satirical comedy, and advertising.

Although its beginning was a little more complicated, *The Man from UNCLE* was conceived quite bluntly as a TV version of James Bond. It became an entity in its own right when development fell to the enormously creative Sam Rolfe, who single-handedly devised the complicated, multi-faceted organisation that was the United Network Command for Law Enforcement—UNCLE. The end result was the most dynamic, complex, fast-paced, action-packed, sexy, and exhilarating adventure show of the 20th century; as the first television series to employ the hand-held camera, the faddish, youth-orientated shows that preceded it moved at a snail's pace in comparison. And with the casting of a co-star who became the most popular MGM actor of all time, *UNCLE* thawed the Cold War and created the buddy movie.

But with the death of President Kennedy, the brave new world of youthful hope and co-operation that the *UNCLE* franchise represented had taken a severe blow. As a result, *The Man from UNCLE* became less of a hopeful dream and more an escapist fantasy in the years to follow. *UNCLE* wanted global peace too, but instead of growing its hair long and throwing flowers around, it wore a dinner suit and used smoke bombs and bullets!

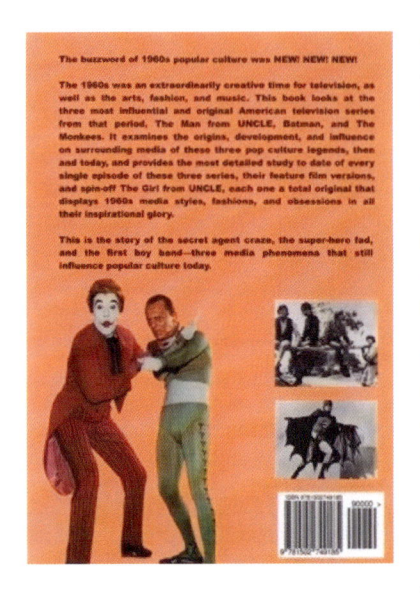

But 1966 was to get wilder still. The *Batman* TV series had arrived in January, 1966 as a mid-season replacement that, following dire test screenings, ABC had no great hopes for. This colorful and stylish parody of the comic-book character delighted kids and adults alike with its bizarre confrontations between the preposterous cowled boy scout Batman and his obnoxious do-gooding student Robin and marvellous performances from familiar Hollywood character actors as the heroes' eccentric adversaries. It became television's second major fad of the 1960s.

The primary legacy of the *Batman* TV series was to give everybody in film and TV permission to go completely loopy, and late '60s film and TV still looks quite bizarre because of it. Nowhere was this more evident than in the wacky TV series *The Monkees,* a half-hour freestyle sit-com imitating the madcap style of the Beatles' feature films. The show was the precursor of the pop video, and the birth of the manufactured boy band, and the onscreen spot gags, parodies, and imaginings of the four leads pre-date series such as *The Simpsons* and *Family Guy* by decades. There had been nothing like these three series before. It would be well over twenty years before anyone dared attempt such levels of creativity again.

These three shows are unique among most television series of any decade in that their influence spread beyond television to affect all aspects of other arts and media as well—books, film, comics, toys, music, satire, fashion, and advertising.

This is the story of the secret agent craze, the super-hero fad, and the first boy band—three media phenomena that still influence popular culture today.

also available from the same author

The Great Desilu TV Series of the 1960s:

a critical celebration of four classic shows

Desi Arnaz and Lucille Ball's imprint is all over television history. The Desilu company that was formed by Lucy and Desi to produce and market Lucy's TV series *I Love Lucy* and *The Lucy Show* was later sold to Paramount, handing them three of the biggest cash cows in television history--for it was Desilu that produced and financed *The Untouchables, Mission: Impossible* and *Star Trek,* three of the most admired and respected television series ever made.

All three would never have made it to air without the power, influence and support of Desi Arnaz and Lucille Ball. It was Lucy who took television out of New York theaterland to Hollywood; she financed the pilot for *I Love Lucy* with her own money; she was the first to film before a live audience; her show pioneered the three camera system of filming sitcoms; her onscreen pregnancy forced American television to grow up a little when it was written into her series. It was Desi who protected *The Untouchables;* it was Lucy who bullied *Star Trek* and *Mission: Impossible* onto the air.

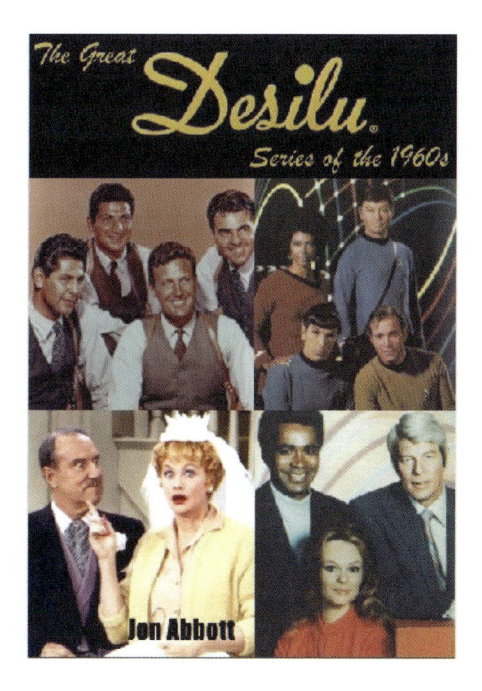

This book examines the four major Desilu legacies of the 1960s in detail-- *The Untouchables, The Lucy Show, Mission: Impossible,* and *Star Trek.*

Controversial mob show *The Untouchables* ran for four seasons (1959 to 1963) until TV's censors and professional complainers finally finished it off. It set the bar so high and created such controversy (albeit media-manufactured) that it was twenty five years before gangster shows of comparable quality appeared, and to this day there has not been a gangland show as successful. It was a pulp paperback brought to life, the American trash magazine as live action TV. The slam-bang rapid pace, the justifiable but shameless voyeuristic violence, and the staccato machine-gun-like narration was unique and exciting in the more slower-paced environment of early-'60s TV, and the list of guest stars giving top-rate performances of mostly first-rate scripts is as long as it is distinguished.

The Lucy Show ran for six seasons, featured wonderful physical comedy, numerous staple sit-com formula plots, and dozens of celebrity guest stars as a significant and popular part of Lucille Ball's twenty year TV career. Her co-stars, Vivian Vance and Gale Gordon (as Mr. Mooney) achieved career highs.

Mission: Impossible was the longest running and most parodied spy show of the 1960s, and is today a major movie franchise. With its dazzling theme, self-destructing taped messages, convoluted schemes, drop-jawed disbelieving villains, and iconic characters, it became a genuine pop culture item.

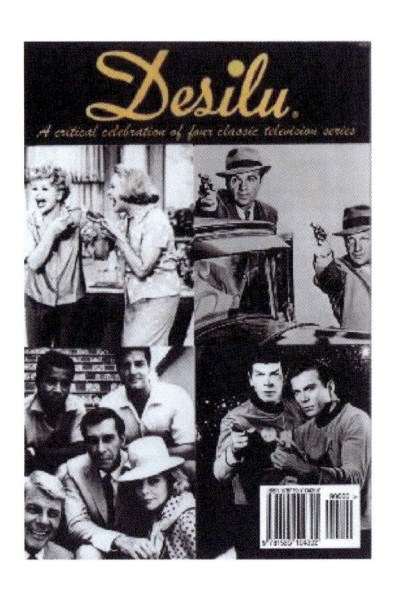

Star Trek, also a major movie franchise, presented pure science-fiction concepts to a mature and wide-ranging mass audience for the first time in television's history, by brilliantly transposing the western formula to futuristic space adventure, and becoming one of the most significant and revered television series in the history of the medium. Desi and Lucy were barely aware they were producing it, but Lucy got it on the air by securing another television first--a second pilot.

The Great Desilu Series of the 1960s is a fascinating, fun-filled, fact-filled story of four famously loved television series--related in the context of each other and discussed together for what I believe to be the first time.

Presented in the same popular format as *Irwin Allen Television Productions* and *Cool TV of the 1960s.*

also available from the same author

Stephen J. Cannell Productions: A History of All Series and Pilots

For twenty years, Stephen J. Cannell was in the hero business. Or perhaps, the anti-hero business. Whatever the case, his heroes were on the side of the slightly tarnished angels.

During the late 1970s and early 1980s, Cannell was the single most influential figure in populist action/adventure television. His series range from the smart, wry humor of *The Rockford Files* to the comic-book exploits of *The A-Team*. In between, he has created, co-created, and overseen such productions as the pacifist but macho war series *Black Sheep Squadron,* superhero spoof *The Greatest American Hero,* the beach boy bromance *Riptide,* the outrageous vigilante show *Hardcastle and McCormick,* and the Eastwood-inspired anti-cop show *Hunter.* In the late '80s, he produced the critically acclaimed *21, Jump Street,* and the quietly horrific, grim, dark mob show *Wiseguy.*

In the 1970s, his marriage of B-western plots and values to the post-Watergate cynicism of 1970s cinema refreshed popular culture, drawing from themes explored and avenues opened by Robert Altman and Clint Eastwood, perhaps the two most influential filmmakers of the period. His knowing, self-parodic approach to a tired and weary action/adventure genre permeated all of American television throughout the 1980s, and much cinema thereafter.

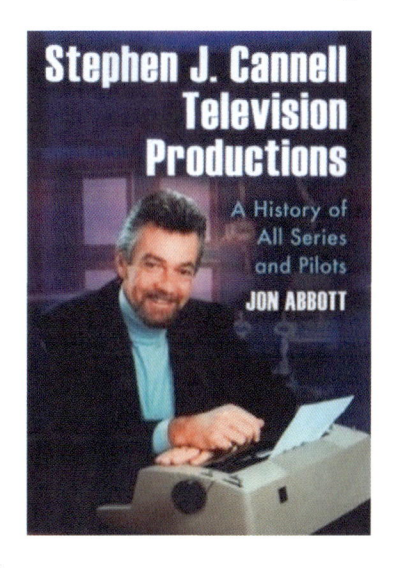

On the surface, Cannell's heroes are traditional conservative icons of Hollywood myth, cops, judges, vigilantes, military men, tough guys--but they are also renegades and rebels, individual malcontents at odds with the injustices of the world. And despite producing shows featuring handsome but flawed male heroes (or perhaps because of it), his shows were phenomenally popular with the female audience as well as the intended men, displaying a satisfying progressive attitude towards women both in front of, and behind the camera.

This book discusses in detail the programs of this writer-producer (and sometimes director and actor), and lists every episode of his 1970s and 1980s series, with storylines and writer, director, and cast credits for 22 shows. With extensive quotes and research, it discusses Cannell's methods of working, his critics, his recurring themes and obsessions, and his successes and failures, and includes publicity materials, information on unsold pilots, and a four-page bibliography and ten pages of sources and quotations to support the author's observations and opinions. Every statement is backed up by cross-referencing numerous examples not only of specific episodes of Cannell shows, but other producers' series as well. There is a 38 page index.

The book features: Part One: Beginnings--*The Rockford Files; Baretta; City of Angels; Black Sheep Squadron; Richie Brockelman; The Duke; Stone;* unsold pilots (one); Part Two: The Golden Years--*Tenspeed and Brownshoe; The Greatest American Hero; The Quest; The A-Team; Hardcastle and McCormick; Rousters; Riptide;* unsold pilots (two); Part Three: From L.A. To Canada--*Hunter; Stingray; The Last Precinct; 21, Jump Street; Wiseguy; J.J. Starbuck; Sonny Spoon; Unsub;* unsold pilots (three); The Wrap-Up (his later series, including *Renegade*); sources of quotations; bibliography; index (all featured series chapters include episode listings).

"Outstanding" (e-mail to publishers, Cannell Entertainment)

also available from the same author

One Hundred of the Best, Most Violent Movies Ever

JON ABBOTT has been writing professionally about 20th century pop culture for over thirty years, with over four hundred articles on TV and film published in over two dozen different magazines, trade, specialist, and populist. Here, he looks at the very best violent movies and their follow-ups before CGI ruined everything and turned action films into second-rate animated computer games.

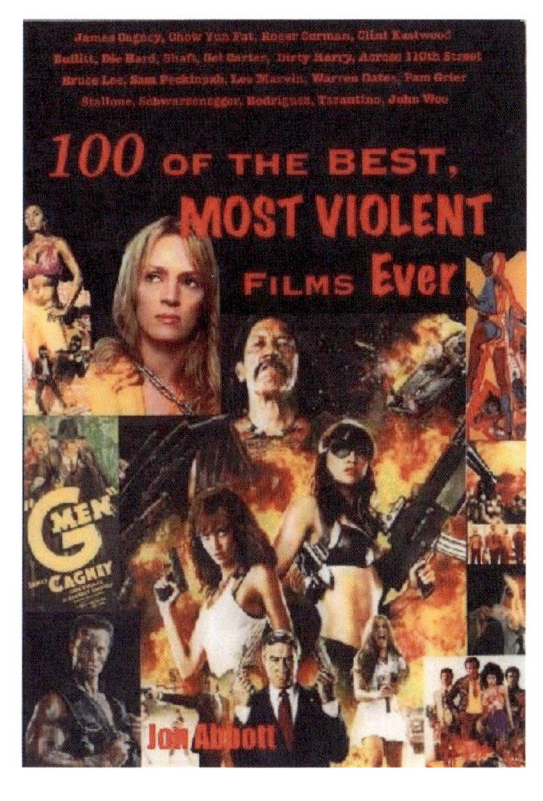

What's the connection between *Star Trek* and *Shaft?* What made William Holden go study his lines? Which 1970s film star was a dead ringer for a 1930s gangster? Which actor from *You Only Live Twice* was attacked by an army of naked ninja girls? What's the film referenced by the glowing case in *Pulp Fiction?* In which film did Pam Grier send her female adversary her boyfriend's, uh, anatomy in a pickle jar? What was the action film set in New York which had Canadian mountains in the background? Who is the action star who one reviewer said "runs like he's covered in bees"? On which gangster film was it easier to get a spliff than a cup of tea? Who ran *The Gauntlet* in a bullet-riddled bus? Which *Coronation Street* star got thrown off the top of a high rise car park? What is the *Kiss of the Dragon?* Which book answers all these questions and gives you even more detail on one hundred of the best action movies ever? Clue: see above!

If it's hypocritical to thoroughly enjoy lurid, violent films yet abhor real violence (as I do), then it seems even more hypocritical to deny the frisson one gets from a violent movie. This book has been written for the pleasure of the audience that shares my enjoyment of the Stallone/Schwarzenegger style of film and their predecessors, and that laughs and hoots along with me as bullet-riddled thugs dance and fall, and buildings and cars explode. I attempted to produce it with the same honesty that I did with *Strange New World,* my study of 1970s sex films, another frowned-upon genre that I enjoy and examined with a complete absence of self-imposed guilt.

From Cagney and Corman to Jackie Chan and Chow Yun Fat, from *Coffy* and *Black Caesar* to *Kill Bill* and *Pulp Fiction,* from Republic serials to the *Die Hards* and their clones, from *Shaft* and *Get Carter* to Schwarzenegger and Stallone, these are films faked the hard way, with real stunts, real explosions, real muscles, real imagination, strong scripts, serious carnage, and real cars on real roads.

Here are one hundred of the best, most violent movies ever. Where they came from, why they're great, and what's in 'em that makes them great.

If one picture is worth a thousand words, what are this lot worth?

also available from the same author

Cool TV 2: More Cult TV from the 1960s

The Sequel Has Landed....

featuring *The Outer Limits, The Invaders, Jonny Quest, The Green Hornet, Burke's Law, Honey West,* and *Amos Burke, Secret Agent*

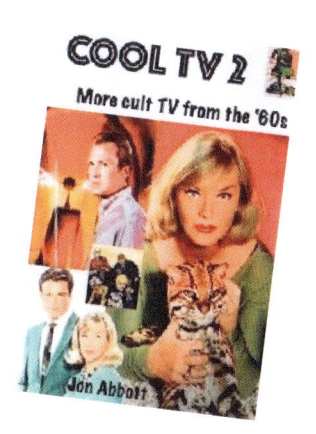

Now, following the successful five star reviewed *Cool TV of the 1960s* comes *Cool TV 2,* featuring all the episodes of seven more cult TV shows from the '60s covered in complete nit-picking, fact-checking, family-annoying, partner-irritating detail: *The Outer Limits, The Invaders, The Green Hornet, Jonny Quest, Burke's Law, Honey West,* and the short-lived, little known *Amos Burke, Secret Agent.*

And check out **The Great Desilu Series of the 1960s**, which gives the same *Cool TV* treatment to *Star Trek, The Untouchables, The Lucy Show,* and *Mission: Impossible...*

Jon Abbott has been writing professionally about 20th century pop culture for over thirty years, during which time he has had over four hundred articles on TV and film published in over two dozen different magazines, trade, specialist, and populist, including *Video Today, Starburst, TV Zone, Dreamwatch, What Satellite, Video Buyer,* and *The DarkSide.* He is currently appearing regularly in *Infinity.*

also available from the same author

The Secret Unseen History of a Television Robin Hood

Okay, now that I've got your attention, here's what this really is. What we have here are some random behind-the-scenes photographs taken during the production of what clearly appears to be the 1955 British television series *The Adventures of Robin Hood.* I stumbled upon them during one of my periodic rambles around the boot fairs and curiosity shops, and as a baby boomer TV and film buff immediately recognised them for what they are.

I present them here without superfluous comment or guesswork, as seen, as a social and historical document for pop culture enthusiasts, TV archivists and social historians, and—if you're the right age—as a nostalgic trip down memory lane. You may have a better idea of what and who the pictures show than I do, as I'm not a personal fan of the show, but as a general enthusiast for the period's television, I remember and recognise Richard Greene, Alexander Gauge, Archie Duncan, and Alan Wheatley. I cherry-picked as many of the best of them that I could afford, and if sales are modest, I might even break even in three or four years, but as a TV historian, I felt they deserved—needed—to be preserved and seen as a valuable record of a part of U.K. TV history and its production process, so I did my duty, rescued them from the damp cardboard box they were scattered in and present them here as found history. Enjoy.

Printed in Poland
by Amazon Fulfillment
Poland Sp. z o.o., Wrocław